Assassinating Hitler

Assassinating Hitler

Ethics and Resistance
in Nazi Germany

Robert Weldon Whalen

Selinsgrove: Susquehanna University Press
London and Toronto: Associated University Presses

Associated University Presses
440 Forsgate Drive
Cranbury, NJ 08512

Associated University Presses
25 Sicilian Avenue
London WC1A 2QH, England

Associated University Presses
P.O. Box 338, Port Credit
Mississauga, Ontario,
Canada L5G 4L8

The paper used in this publication meets the requirements
of the American National Standard for Permanence of Paper
for Printed Library Materials Z39.48-1984.

Library of Congress Cataloging-in-Publication Data

Whalen, Robert Weldon, 1950–
    Assassinating Hitler : ethics and resistance in Nazi Germany /
Robert Weldon Whalen.
        p.   cm.
    Includes bibliographical references and index.
    ISBN 0-945636-45-8 (alk. paper)
    1. Hitler, Adolf, 1889–1945—Assassination attempt, 1944 (July
20)—Moral and ethical aspects.   2. World War, 1939–1945—
Underground movements.   I. Title.
DD256.35.W47   1993
943.086—dc20   92-56704
                                                                CIP

Selections from Friedrich Reck-Malleczewen, *Diary of a Man in Despair* are reprinted with the permission of Macmillan Publishing Company. English translation copyright 1970 by Paul Rubens.

Selections from Dietrich Bonhoeffer are reprinted from *Letters and Papers from Prison*, revised, enlarged edition, by Dietrich Bonhoeffer, translated from the German by Reginald Fuller, Frank Clark, et al., English translation copyright 1953, 1967, 1971, with the permission of Macmillan Publishing Company and SCM Press, Ltd.

PRINTED IN THE UNITED STATES OF AMERICA

For Meg . . .

A Klee painting named "Angelus Novus" shows an angel looking as though he is about to move away from something he is fixedly contemplating. His eyes are staring, his mouth is open, his wings are spread. This is how one pictures the angel of history. His face is turned toward the past. Where we perceive a chain of events, he sees one single catastrophe which keeps piling wreckage upon wreckage and hurls it in front of his feet. The angel would like to stay, awaken the dead, and make whole what has been smashed. But a storm is blowing from Paradise; it has got caught in his wings with such violence that the angel can no longer close them. This storm irresistibly propels him into the future to which his back is turned, while the pile of debris before him grows skyward. This storm is what we call progress.

—Walter Benjamin, "Theses on the Philosophy of History"

Contents

Acknowledgments

Books take a long time to write, and this book is no exception. During its writing, many people have offered suggestions, criticisms, and above all, encouragement, and I want to thank them. They are not, of course, responsible for the content of this book, nor do they necessarily agree with it. But without their help it would never have come to fruition.

The inspiration for this book came largely from my work with Isabel Hull and John Weiss of Cornell University. Its progress was encouraged by my colleagues at Queens College, especially William Thompson, Molly Davis, Norris Preyer, Robert Porter, Charles Reed, Richard Goode, Bari Watkins, and Billy O. Wireman. The Carolyn G. and Sam H. McMahon Jr. professorship at Queens College provided welcome support for this project.

I wish to thank as well Director Hans Feldmann of Susquehanna University Press and Thomas Yoseloff and Michael Koy of Associated University Presses, and their colleagues, for their help with this work. They are the people who brought this book to print; without their professional skill and good faith, it would not exist.

This book speaks about love and honor, faith and family. What I have learned about these things, I have learned not so much from books as from my parents, Weldon and Genevieve Whalen. My debt to them is greater than my telling and far beyond my repaying. My mother did not live to see this book's completion, but I finish these final pages with her memory strong in my heart and with the hope that this book will honor her. My brother, Rev. David M. Whalen, O.S.F.S., deserves many thanks too for his constant encouragement of my work.

Meg Freeman Whalen, my wife, counselor, and best friend, has taken much time from her own work to hearten me and this book along our often tangled way. It could not have appeared without her. That is why this book is for Meg.

Dramatis Personae

LUDWIG BECK (1880–1944). Professional soldier. Resigned as chief of the General Staff in 1938, and became the leader of resistance movement, which culminated in the 20 July 1944, assassination and coup attempt. Executed, following a suicide attempt, on the night of 20 July.

DIETRICH BONHOEFFER (1906–45). Lutheran pastor and theologian. Member of the Abwehr (German Military Intelligence) resistance group. Imprisoned in April 1943; executed in April 1945.

WILHELM CANARIS (1887–1945). Admiral, chief of the Abwehr, German Military Intelligence. Protected his deputy, General Hans Oster, who turned the Abwehr into a center of the conservative resistance. Executed in April 1945.

ALFRED DELP (1907–45). A Jesuit priest, member of Helmuth James von Moltke's Kreisau Circle. Executed in 1945.

HANS VON DOHNANYI (1902–45). Lawyer and civil servant; Bonhoeffer's brother-in-law. The Abwehr's legal counsel, and key Abwehr conspirator. Arrested in 1943; executed in 1945.

HANS BERND GISEVIUS (1905–74). Lawyer and civil servant, he became the Abwehr's contact with Allied Intelligence in Switzerland. Present in Berlin during the 20 July coup attempt, he managed to escape. He was one of the conspiracy's few survivors.

CARL GOERDELER (1884–1945). Civil servant, former mayor of Leipzig. An old-school patriot and nationalist, he was the conservative resistance's tireless propagandist. Arrested in August 1944; executed in February 1945.

HANS-BERND VON HAEFTEN (1904–44). Civil servant and diplomat. A leader of the resistance in the Foreign Office. Executed in 1944.

11

WERNER VON HAEFTEN (1909–44). Hans-Bernd von Haeften's brother and Claus von Stauffenberg's aide. He accompanied Stauffenberg on the mission to kill Hitler on 20 July 1944. Executed on the night of 20 July.

ULRICH VON HASSELL (1881–1944). Professional diplomat. With Goerdeler and Beck, one of the leaders of the older circle of the conservative resistance. His diaries are a key record of the resistance. Executed in 1944.

CÄSAR VON HOFACKER (1896–1944). Soldier, related to the Stauffenbergs. Organizer of the military resistance in Paris. Executed in 1944.

JULIUS LEBER (1891–1945). Social democratic politician and labor leader. One of the leading political leftists associated with the 20 July Plot. Executed in 1945.

HELMUTH JAMES VON MOLTKE (1907–45). Lawyer, legal advisor to the Abwehr, organizer of the Kreisau Circle resistance group. Executed in 1945.

FRIEDRICH OLBRICHT (1888–1944). Professional soldier. Chief of the logistic division of the Reserve Army and one of the technicians of the Plot. Executed on the night of 20 July.

HANS OSTER (1888–1945). Professional soldier. Deputy director of the Abwehr; one of the principal organizers of the conservative resistance. Executed in 1945.

FRIEDRICH PERCYVAL RECK-MALLECZEWEN (1884–1945). A conservative Prussian, he was not a member of the conspiracy. His wartime diary, however, reflects the values of the conservative anti-Nazis. Executed in 1945.

FABIAN VON SCHLABRENDORFF (1907–80). Lawyer. Served on the staff of General Henning von Tresckow, and was the liaison between Tresckow's group and the Berlin conspirators. He survived the war and wrote one of the earliest reports of the conspiracy.

FRIEDRICH WERNER VON DER SCHULENBURG (1875–1944). Diplomat, from 1935–41, German ambassador to the Soviet Union. Diplomatic advisor to the conservative resistance. Executed in 1944.

FRITZ-DIETLOF VON DER SCHULENBURG (1902–44). Nephew of Friedrich Werner von der Schulenberg. Lawyer and civil servant. At one time, an enthusiastic member of the Nazi Party, he turned against the party and became an active resister. Executed in 1944.

BERTHOLD SCHENK VON STAUFFENBERG (1905–44). Lawyer and diplomat. In 1944, a lawyer for the navy and one of the Plot's planners. Executed in 1944.

CLAUS SCHENK VON STAUFFENBERG (1907–44). Berthold's brother. The "trigger" of the conspiracy. Executed on the night of 20 July.

HENNING VON TRESCKOW (1904–44). Professional soldier. Organizer of the resistance among staff officers on the Russian Front. Committed suicide in 1944.

ADAM VON TROTT ZU SOLZ (1909–44). Professional diplomat and member of the Abwehr. Executed in 1944.

MARIE ("MISSIE") VASSILTCHIKOV (1917–78). Daughter of an aristocratic Russian family, as a young woman she worked for Adam Trott zu Solz in the Foreign Office, and knew many of the July 20 conspirators. Her diary is an important record of wartime Berlin and the conspiracy.

ERWIN VON WITZLEBEN (1881–1944). Professional soldier. Named commander of the Army by the conspirators. Executed in 1944.

PETER YORCK VON WARTENBURG (1904–44). Lawyer and civil servant. Relative of the Stauffenbergs. Member of Helmuth James von Moltke's Kreisau Circle. Executed in 1944.

Assassinating Hitler

Prologue: Resistance and Civic Virtue

> Maybe one day we will be happy to think about even these
> things.
>
> —Vergil

This is a book about what Edmund Burke called the "moral
imagination," that "wardrobe" which contains all the "decent
drapery of life," the "superadded ideas . . . which the heart owns
and the understanding ratifies, as necessary to cover the defects
of our naked shivering nature, and to raise it to dignity."[1] Its
focus is the moral imagination of those soldiers and civilians
who, in July 1944, attempted, in what they called "Operation
Valkyrie," to kill Adolf Hitler, seize power, and end the Second
World War. This book is essentially not a definitive study, but a
raid, a reconnaissance, an exploration.

The aim of this book is not to introduce new sources, but to
ask new questions of old sources. The historian's first task is to
unearth unknown materials, but the historian's work does not
end there. As H. Stuart Hughes remarks in another context:

> Historians in this country [the United States] seem to have forgot-
> ten—if they ever learned properly—the simple truth that what one
> may call progress in their endeavors comes not merely through the
> discovery of new materials but at least as much through a new read-
> ing of materials already available.[2]

This book attempts such a new reading of old materials in an
effort to reexamine an old question: When love of country and
love of virtue collide, how shall we know what to do, and even
when we know what to do, how do we muster the courage to do
what we must?

That virtue and politics are, or should be, related, no one disputes. Just how virtue and politics are related is, however, a point
of considerable confusion. In 1984, for example, a West German
general was implicated in a sordid sex and spy scandal. He gave

17

his "word of honor" that he was innocent. *Die Zeit* felt obliged to explain to its readers just what in the world a "word of honor" was—the article, by Theodor Eschenburg, was appropriately entitled, "The Obsolete 'Word of Honor.'"[3] "What Ever Happened to Ethics?" asked the cover of *Time* magazine plaintively in May 1987; *Time* then devoted some fifteen pages to an examination of the United States's troubled search for "its moral bearings."[4] Robert Bellah and his colleagues in *Habits of the Heart* write that at least among Americans, questions of virtue are very important, but that "concern about moral questions is often relegated to the realm of private anxiety, as if it would be awkward or embarrassing to make them public."[5] In our "naked public square,"[6] in our ironic age of "anti-heroes,"[7] in a "narcissistic" era[8] in which private urges overwhelm public imperatives,[9] we find it hard not only to talk about politics and virtue, but to talk about talking about politics and virtue; in our time, Virginia Woolf writes, "we have no ceremonies, only private dirges and no conclusions, only violent sensations, each separate."[10] It is well in an age obsessed with survival,[11] however, to remember that mere survival is not really the ultimate issue. "You are mistaken," Socrates argues,

> . . . if you think that someone who is worth anything ought to spend time weighing up the prospects of life and death. One ought to consider one thing only . . . whether one is acting rightly or wrongly, like a good citizen or a bad one . . . the difficulty is not so much to escape death; the real difficulty is to escape from doing wrong.[12]

Trying to understand politics and virtue is an old task. It was, after all, Cicero, in 49 B.C., who asked the question that haunted the July 20 Conspirators:

> Should one stay in one's country even if it is under totalitarian rule? Is it justifiable to use any means to end such rule, if those means endanger the whole fabric of the state? Is it statesmanlike, when one's country is under a tyrant, to return to some other place and remain inactive there, or ought one to brave any danger in order to liberate it?[13]

History can help us answer Cicero's questions. Memory, as the ancient historians knew, is a powerful teacher, and what historical memory should teach, they thought, is civic virtue. "This above all makes history useful and valuable," according to Livy. "It unfolds before our eyes the illustrious record of exemplary action." And Tacitus writes: "To me, the chief duty of the historian is this: to see that virtue is placed on record, that evil people and evil deeds may have cause to fear the judgment of posterity."[14] Karl Jaspers reminds us: "What and how we remember . . . will help determine what we become."[15]

Studying the July 20 Conspiracy can help, too. It is, to be sure, an exception, a "border situation," an occasion of "shipwreck," but it is precisely the incandescence of the extreme that can enlighten the routines of the mundane.

Hans Rothfels, in one of the first studies of the July 20 Conspiracy, insisted on its essentially moral dimension:

> No examination of the German opposition to Hitler will succeed which limits itself to the narrow sphere of political opinions and possibilities, which limits itself to sociological or psychoanlaytical investigation of "class" motives of the "old elite," or to the "nationalist" goals of the resistance. . . . Such a so-called "realist" approach may be useful in certain cases. But to see the essence of the thing, one must probe to principles, to the moral issues.[16]

Three decades after Rothfels's study, Peter Hoffman, the conspiracy's most expert student, made precisely the same point: "[The conspiracy] can only be understood from the inside: the drive to opposition, provoked by conscience, is the kernel of and key to the entire event; if this is not recognized, nothing about the conspiracy can be understood."[17] Virtually everyone who has studied the conspiracy has agreed that moral imperatives were at the heart of the affair, and yet, there still is no systematic investigation of the conspirators' moral universe.[18]

This book attempts to excavate the conspirators' moral world, but also to embed it in the density of their own experience. The historian's most elementary task is to recreate imaginatively his or her subject's world, but many of the studies of 20 July obscure or ignore the peculiar dynamics and tensions of the conspirators' world. In 1984, for example, the Historical Commission of the City of Berlin sponsored an international conference on the July 20 Conspiracy. Scholars discussed every dimension of the conspiracy, including "political and moral motivations," and the published papers and comments add up to some 1,185 pages. Yet something was missing. Marianne Meyer-Krahmer, Carl Goerdeler's daughter, remarked that the "cold, analytical discussions" gave her, as one who had lived through the conspiracy, the odd sense of "having her back against the wall." Because no one

seemed to understand the passions and values of the conspirators, there seemed little effort to recapture the context of the
conspirators' lives.[19] This book will try to represent those passions and values earlier studies have missed.

Exploring the moral imagination of the July 20 Conspirators
is no easy task. The 20 July plotters deceived and were deceived;
they compromised their honor, and killed to regain it. The July
20 Conspiracy encourages and yet provokes. Protean, it not only
changes with the perspective of the observer, but it also changes
the perspectives of the observer. In the summer of 1944, just after
the coup, Missie Vassiltchikov, a young secretary in the German
Foreign Office who was well acquainted with many of the conspirators, agreed to shelter a male friend who was reluctant to
go home during an air raid. Missie's old cook was scandalized,
and her comment has more than anecdotal value: "In my younger
days, that couldn't have happened, but this 20th July has turned
everything topsy-turvy."[20] The student of the conspiracy can only
sympathize with the anonymous Gestapo bureaucrat who observed five decades ago: "This 20th of July is getting beyond us.
We can't control the thing any longer."[21]

Chapter 1, Valkyrie, narrates the climactic event of the July 20
Conspiracy —Operation Valkyrie—the assassination and coup
attempt of July 1944. The second chapter, Vermächtnis ("legacy"), outlines the often angry debate that has raged since 1945
about the meaning of Valkyrie. The remaining chapters explore
the dimensions of the conspirators' moral imagination: Chara-
kter, discusses the conspirators' personalities; Vettern ("kin") examines their family relationships; Ehre ("honor") explores their
distinctive understanding of honor; Anti-Christ analyzes their
encounter with the moral evil of the Hitler regime; and finally
Gewissen ("conscience") outlines the structure of their moral
imagination, particularly within the context of Christian ethics.
The epitaph, Gewitteraktion ("Operation 'Thunderstorm'") explains the price the Nazis exacted of the conspirators, and concludes the book's analysis.

The conspirators' moral imagination might seem peculiar, but
it is well to remember that it was shaped by peculiar times. The
anti-Nazi underground was unavoidably textured by the Third
Reich, and that, as Michael Balfour reminds us, was a "very peculiar place" indeed;[22] it was Burke's "antagonistic world" of "mad-
ness, discord, vice, confusion, and unavailing sorrow."[23] Entry
into the underground was dangerous, movement through its
labyrinths treacherous, and exit all but impossible. The conspira-

tors did not so much inhabit the underground as it inhabited them. In April 1940, for example, Helmuth James von Moltke, the organizer of the anti-Nazi Kreisau Circle, wrote to his wife:

April 18th, 1940. Last night, I had a disturbing dream. I was sent on duty to Holland and had a free weekend. Whereupon I decided to go to London with an American passport belonging to a friend who otherwise did not figure in the dream. . . . For some unexplained reason I missed the train which would have got me back to the Hague in time for work on Monday. And with that an otherwise nice dream came to an unpleasant end. I found myself confronted with the need to choose between two alternatives—either to be shot in England as a spy, or in Germany as a traitor.[24]

Yet the underground, though drama, was no dream. It existed in our own time, only a generation ago. As we explore it, we must remember that, like Shakespearian tragedy, it occurred not in the heavens but here, among us, "on earth, the cruelest of planets."[25]

1
Valkyrie

TOP SECRET.
20 July 1944
Message 1.
1. The Führer Adolf Hitler is dead. . . .

Message 3.
1. . . .
2. The following measures are to be taken immediately . . .
(b) Arrests: the following are to be placed in secure solitary confinement: all Gauleiter . . . [and] senior SS and Gestapo officials. . . .
(c) Concentration camps will be occupied at once, camp commanders arrested, guard personnel disarmed. . . .
5. In the exercise of executive power, no arbitrary acts or acts of revenge will be tolerated. The people must be made aware of the difference from the arbitrary methods of their former rulers.

/signed/ Stauffenberg[1]

Just past dawn on Thursday, 20 July 1944, Claus von Stauffenberg and his brother, Berthold, awoke and dressed. They lived in Tristian Strasse, Wahnsee, in Berlin's West End. It was Berthold's home; Claus had been stationed in Berlin the autumn before, and had moved in with his brother. Their wives and children lived in southern Germany, safe from Allied bombers.

Berthold put on his navy uniform. In civilian life, Berthold was an international lawyer; now, during the war, he was a Navy judge. Berthold was thirty-eight years old in 1944. He was the introvert of the family, shy, scholarly, taciturn.

Claus, the family extrovert, was thirty-six years old; he would turn thirty-seven in November. He was slower in dressing. In April 1943, while serving in North Africa, he had been badly wounded, and had lost his left eye, two fingers on his left hand, and much of his right arm. But he had recovered quickly, and

was proud of his ability to care for himself. His wife, Nina, recalled that while Claus was recovering, in the summer of 1943:

> He refused to take any pain-killers. He was proud of physical inde-
> pendence, and learned to eat and shave and wash with just the three
> fingers on his left hand. Once, he insisted on tying the belt around
> his robe, just to prove that he could do it.[2]

Claus Phillip Maria Schenk Graf von Stauffenberg was known
as one of the brightest young colonels on the German General
Staff; he was a dynamo, with an infectious laugh. Stauffenberg
was a remarkably handsome man, with thin, angular features;
his empty sleeve and eye-patch gave him a piratical look. To some
of his colleagues, Claus von Stauffenberg was an indefatigable
devil's advocate, with a gift for sarcasm. "Do you know why I
have this picture in my office?" he asked friends in the winter
of 1941–42, pointing to an enormous portrait of Adolf Hitler.
"I've picked this one so that everyone who comes to my office
gets some sense of lunacy and dizzying disproportion."[3]

He could be both secretive and ruthlessly blunt. In 1943, for
example, he called Lieutenant Urban Thiersch into his office. To
the younger men, Stauffenberg seemed to be the model staff officer staff. But on that day, the young officer later recounted:

> "Let us go 'in media res,'" Stauffenberg said. . . . "I am plotting high
> treason. . . ." He earnestly added that it was questionable whether it
> would succeed, but that far worse than failure would be to bow before
> shame and coercion. Only by acting could we win inner, and outer,
> freedom.

Lieutenant Thiersch agreed to help.[4]

In the early years of the war, Stauffenberg was convinced that
if someone would only confront Hitler with the truth about war
crimes and incompetent leadership, the führer would surely take
corrective action. "It's scandalous," he insisted in the fall of
1942, "that at a time when millions of soldiers daily risk their
lives, not a single commander is willing to stand up to the Führer, take off his helmet, and tell him the truth—even if it cost the
commander his life."[5]

But by the following year, Stauffenberg's optimism about the
führer had distintegrated. Later, when asked what should be
done about the führer, Stauffenberg answered: "Kill him."[6] By
then, as his uncle, Nicholas Uxküll, remembered, Claus had become the "trigger" of the conspiracy.[7] Yet what others remem-

bered about Stauffenberg were his good humor, his laughter, and a courtesy sometimes so theatrical that it made brother officers smile.[8]

That morning, 20 July 1944, Claus von Stauffenberg dressed in his General Staff uniform. He wore a chain around his neck with a small cross attached, a gift from his wife. He wore a small ring as well with the cryptic inscription "finis-initium," which might be translated "end-beginning."[9]

Colonel von Stauffenberg was chief of staff of the Reserve Army, the organization responsible, among other things, for training replacements for the Army. He had a plane to catch on 20 July. On the day before, he had been ordered to fly to the führer's East Prussian headquarters, the Wolf's Lair, to brief the führer on reinforcements available for the Russian Front.

Thursday, 20 July, would be a warm day.[10] Most of the world was absorbed, that day, as were the Stauffenberg brothers, with the World War, then in its fifth year. New York papers reported fierce fighting in Normandy, an immense Russian offensive, and rocket attacks on London. It was humid in New York too; the *New York Times* warned its readers to prepare for thunderstorms. The *London Times*, that Thursday, reported on a "Monstrous Offer" made by the Germans, to trade Hungarian Jews to the Allies in exchange for munitions.

But the world was thinking about the end of the war, too. In Britain, Parliament debated postwar housing policy. The Swiss argued about an "exiles tax"—the idea was that people who had fled Switzerland during the war and then returned ought to pay a special tax as a kind of penalty for desertion. In Chicago, the final session of the Democratic National Convention was scheduled for that evening. Franklin Roosevelt would be nominated for an extraordinary fourth term; Harry Truman would be nominated as his vice president.[11]

The Stauffenberg brothers were also thinking about the end of the war. Claus would, that day, end the war by killing Adolf Hitler. The assassination would trigger a military coup d'état, and the new government would liquidate the Third Reich. Before that sultry Thursday was done, Hitler would be dead; the Nazis' power broken; an anti-Nazi government would be in power in Germany; and the war would be all but over; or the Stauffenbergs, and many others, would be dead.

Corporal Karl Schweizer drove up in a military sedan to the Stauffenberg's home just after 6:00 A.M. He drove the brothers through Berlin's rubbled streets, south, to Rangsdorf Airfield. On the way, he picked up Claus's young aide, Werner von Haeften. Haeften, like Stauffenberg, was a wounded veteran. Normally, Haeften picked Stauffenberg up in the morning and drove him to Reserve Army's headquarters in downtown Berlin, on Bendlerstrasse, just off the Tiergarten. Haeften was a cheerful young man, thirty-six years old in 1944, who typically waved at fellow officers as he and Stauffenberg drove to work. His brother, Hans-Bernd, worked in the Foreign Office; both Hans-Bernd and Werner were conspirators. People remembered later that Werner von Haeften, though still cheerful, seemed especially preoccupied that summer of 1944.[12] Missie Vassiltchikov, the twenty-seven-year-old aristocratic Russian exile who worked for Adam Trott zu Solz in the Foreign Office, wrote in her diary when she learned of the coup attempt:

Thursday, July 20, 1944. . . . I had met young Haeften at Adam Trott's a couple of months ago. One evening, when I was dining with Adam alone, a curly-headed, good-looking young captain had burst in, introduced himself and dragged Adam out of the room. They had stayed away for a long time. Afterwards, Adam was curious to know what impression he had made on me. I answered: "The typical conspirator, such as one reads about in children's books."[13]

The staff car arrived at Rangsdorf Airfield around 7:00 A.M. The drive through Berlin was eerie. Train stations were constantly in chaos, much of Berlin itself was in rubble; the city, because of incessant Allied bombing, seemed perpetually enveloped in smoke. Sometimes, after a heavy bombing, fires made the entire city glow crimson in the night. On 23 November 1943, Missie Vassiltchikov wrote in her diary: "Last night, the greater part of central Berlin was destroyed . . . the sky on three sides was blood-red," and on 19 July 1944, she wrote: "We reached Berlin at eleven, but owing to recent air-raids all stations are in a state of chaos . . . the town is enveloped in smoke; there is rubble everywhere."[14]

When they reached Rangsdorf, the courier plane, a Henkel-111, was ready to leave. General Helmut Stieff was waiting at Rangsdorf. Stieff was one of the many officers assigned to Hitler's headquarters. He had the distinction of being the shortest officer in the German army. He was also a conspirator.

The men chatted briefly. Claus said good-bye to Berthold, who drove with Corporal Schweizer to Navy headquarters. Then Stauffenberg, Haeften, and Stieff climbed aboard the plane. They carried brief cases; Stauffenberg's was tawny leather, almost yellow. Inside, concealed by his papers, were a pliers and two bombs. Stauffenberg would use the pliers to prime the bombs that would kill Hitler and anyone near him.

The plane took off about 7:30 A.M. On that clear summer morning the flight to East Prussia was easy but long. It was some 560 kilometers to the airstrip at Rastenburg, which served Hitler's headquarters, the Wolf's Lair. The flight would take around three hours.

That morning, while Stauffenberg was underway, conspirators in the Army's command complex at Zossen, just outside Berlin, began alerting contacts at key commands. They passed along a single codeword, "Übung" (exercise). "Übung" meant that the assassination of the commander-in-chief was imminent.

The plane landed at the Rastenburg airfield just after 11:00 A.M. A waiting staff car drove Stauffenberg, Haeften, and Stieff down the forest trails to the Wolf's Lair. The Wolf's Lair was a big installation, sprawling over some three square kilometers. Wire and mine fields surrounded its periphery. Inside, top security areas were enclosed by barbed wire.[15] The staff car passed through the outer gate and drove down the gravel path, past huts and barracks, to the camp headquarters. Stieff and Haeften went off on errands; Stauffenberg stayed at the camp headquarters, had a late breakfast, and chatted with friends. He seemed to be in his usual good humor.

Around noon, Field Marshal Wilhelm Keitel, the führer's chief of staff, came looking for Stauffenberg. Keitel's lot was not a happy one. Hitler had promoted him precisely because he was pliable, and his fellow officers nicknamed him "Gummilöwe," meaning the "rubber lion." More unkindly he was known simply as Hitler's "stooge."[16] He walked a bit like a fretting accountant,[17] and today he was especially nervous. Mussolini was coming, and the führer's briefing had been moved up to 12:30 P.M. Stauffenberg was scheduled to brief Hitler on reinforcements for the Eastern Front, and he would have to hurry.

Stauffenberg said he wouldn't be a minute, but that he wanted to freshen up, quickly change his shirt; it was a sweaty day after all, and his aide, Haeften, would help. While Keitel fidgeted, Stauffenberg and Haeften stepped into a side-room, and opened their briefcases. They took out the two bombs.

The things had to be primed. A small ampule of acid had to be squeezed with a pliers and ruptured. The acid would silently eat through a wire that held the trigger. When the wire broke, the trigger would explode the bomb. Once the acid was released, the bomb would go off in about ten minutes.

The plan was to use two bombs. Stauffenberg grasped a specially twisted pliers in his crippled hand and primed the first bomb. He placed it in his briefcase.[18]

Suddenly a sergeant popped his head into the room—"Would the colonel please hurry?" The sergeant looked at the two men, and the open briefcases, and the odd things wrapped in brown paper, and left.

There was no time now for the second bomb, one would have to do. Haeften stuffed the unprimed bomb back in his briefcase and hurried off to arrange for a car for their departure.

Stauffenberg grasped his briefcase and caught up with the impatient Keitel. One of the officers in Keitel's entourage offered to help Stauffenberg with the briefcase. Stauffenberg replied pleasantly that he could manage quite well; as they approached the briefing hut, though, he did accept help with the briefcase, and asked to be placed as near as possible to the führer.

The bomb would explode in about five minutes.

They were late. When they entered the barracks and hurried down the corridor, they could hear General Adolf Heusinger briefing Hitler about the Eastern Front. As they walked past the communications office, Stauffenberg whispered something to a soldier about expecting a telephone call.

They quietly entered the room. Hitler was directly in front of them, his back toward them, standing at the side of a heavy oak table. On the table was a immense map of eastern Europe and the Soviet Union. Around the table were a dozen or so officers.

Lieutenants and sergeants tiptoed softly in and out. Keitel quietly introduced Stauffenberg to Hitler as Heusinger droned on. It was just past 12:30 P.M.

Heusinger was at Hitler's immediate right. Stauffenberg squeezed in at Heusinger's right, so close to Hitler that he could almost touch him. Stauffenberg slid his tan briefcase under the table. Heusinger pointed out towns and fronts and roads and divisions; Hitler leaned over the heavy table, following Heusinger's marks on the map.[19]

Stauffenberg muttered something about a telephone call to the officer on his right and briskly left the room. He did not stop at the communications office. The telephone sergeant watched him hurry by; his black eye-patch made him unmistakable.

Stauffenberg stepped into the bright July sunshine, the day

was humid, the sky was blue, he walked down a gravel path, through the gate in the fence that protected the briefing area, to a waiting staff car. Haeften was with the car. A young lieutenant was at the wheel.

At about 12:40 P.M., with a sudden sharp bang, the bomb exploded.

The bomb's blast stunned some people around the Wolf's Lair. Later they said it sounded like a 150-millimeter artillery shell detonating; some said they thought it was an air raid. Acrid smoke billowed from the briefing hut.

But such noises were hardly rare in wartime. Troops often test-fired explosives. Animals sometimes set off the land mines that surrounded the headquarters. Even people close to the briefing hut noticed nothing strange at first.

That momentary confusion gave Stauffenberg and Haeften the time they needed. As soon as they heard the blast, they hurried into the staff car. Stauffenberg ordered the lieutenant to drive to the airfield.

They drove through the Wolf's Lair, which was still humming with routine activity and still unaware of the explosion at its heart. They drove past knots of soldiers and staff officers going about their business. They were stopped at the exit from the top security area, but Stauffenberg's brusk general staff officer's tone convinced the guard to wave them on.

At the outer gate they were stopped again. The guard had just received a telephone call. Something had happened, and the guard was nervous. He would not let anyone leave. Stauffenberg calmly stepped out of the car, and called a friend at camp headquarters. The friend assured the guard that it was all right to let Colonel Stauffenberg and his aide pass. The guard stepped back and waved them on.

Back down the trail they drove, through the green and bright East Prussian forest. In his rearview mirror, the driver noticed that Haeften fished something wrapped in brown paper out of his briefcase and pitched it out the window into the brush.[20]

They were back at the airfield by 1:00 P.M. The Berlin courier plane was waiting. Stauffenberg and Haeften hurried aboard. The plane rumbled down the airstrip and climbed into the blue summer sky.

The bomb had gone off with a clap of thunder and a blinding flash and had split the heavy briefing table in two, shattering the briefing room, killing two people to Hitler's immediate right, mortally wounding two others, and injuring another dozen people. Through the smoke and rubble, dazed, deafened, covered with blood, men stumbled from the briefing barracks. Keitel was pulling and dragging Hitler.

Keitel hurried the führer to his personal physician. Hitler was dazed but still conscious. He was stained with smoke, his eardrums were ruptured, his trousers were in shreds, and his legs were flecked with blood. He was temporarily deafened. He had suffered bruises and cuts, and his right arm throbbed.

The bomb had gone off not five feet from him. It had killed or wounded some twenty people. It had barely touched him.[21]

General Erich Fellgiebel's call came through to Bendlerstrasse just after 1:00 P.M. Fellgiebel was the director of telecommunications at the Wolf's Lair. He was also a conspirator. His mission was to alert the other conspirators of the assassination, and then cut all links with Hitler's headquarters. He had already alerted several other conspirators.

At the Bendlerstrasse, the headquarters of the Reserve Army, he spoke briefly with Wilhelm Thiele. The attempt had been made, but it seemed that Hitler had survived.

And that message placed the Bendlerstrasse conspirators in an impossible situation. Friedrich Olbricht, director of the General Army Office, and one of the key conspirators, had to decide what to do. Had Hitler been killed, Olbricht was to launch *Operation Valkyrie*. *Valkyrie* directed army commanders throughout Germany to seize power. It was a perfectly legitimate military operation. *Valkyrie* had been prepared two years before, and was designed to be implemented in case of an internal emergency, such as rioting by concentration camp inmates or the millions of foreign workers toiling in German factories. In 1943, however, the conspirators hijacked the plan. Olbricht, Stauffenberg, Henning von Tresckow, and others had secretly modified the operation so that once launched it would be, in effect, a military coup. And they, the conspirators, would lead the coup.

Hitler's assassination was vital to *Valkyrie*. With Hitler dead, the Nazi machine would be in chaos, at least temporarily, and in that brief confusion, the conspirators would have at least a chance to seize power. Stauffenberg had a vital double role in the coup. As chief of staff of the Reserve Army, he alone among the conspirators had the authority to direct *Valkyrie*. Olbricht and others could issue the *Valkyrie* orders, but if Stauffenberg did not endorse them, the commanders in the field most likely would not obey them. Of the conspirators, only Stauffenberg had personal access to Hitler, and only Stauffenberg could kill him. Stauffenberg, then, had to commit the assassination, and then direct the coup. It was an all but impossible plan, but there was no alternative.

Less than a week before, Stauffenberg had flown to Berchtesgaden to plant the bomb, and Olbricht had issued warning orders for *Valkyrie*. But Stauffenberg had decided not to explode the bomb because Goering and Himmler were not at the meeting, and Stauffenberg hoped to kill them with Hitler. At the last moment, Stauffenberg canceled the operation, and Olbricht had to explain lamely to confused commanders that the *Valkyrie* orders had simply been a drill.

The conspiracy's cover had very nearly been blown. Now, on the afternoon of 20 July, Olbricht huddled with Thiele and Albrecht Mertz von Quirnheim, one of Stauffenberg's closest friends. The three officers tried to make sense of the situation. Mertz urged Olbricht to launch *Valkyrie*. Olbricht refused. They would have to wait. If something had gone wrong, they could not risk the entire conspiracy. They had to wait. They must not do anything suspicious. Everyone should continue with his normal routine.

The little conference broke up. Olbricht stepped from the building. Perhaps to catch his breath, or perhaps, knowing the coup's likely outcome, there was some last thing he needed to do.[22]

Mertz paused, but only for a few moments. He could not issue *Valkyrie* himself, but he could issue a preliminary warning order. He walked up to the second floor to the little communications office. There were civilian secretaries in the room, supervised by a sergeant, and tele-typewriters, printers, and telephones. Mertz told them to alert all commands that a critical order was imminent. It was about 2:00 P.M.[23]

When Friedrich Olbricht returned and learned what Mertz had done, he was furious. Later he remarked that "Mertz has railroaded me."[24] Olbricht may have been angry with Mertz, but he had no intention of abandoning the conspiracy, and now there was no turning back. Olbricht and Mertz issued further orders for *Valkyrie*, and while Mertz started briefing the other officers in the Bendlerstrasse, Olbricht reported to General Fritz Fromm, the commander of the Reserve Army.

The führer, Olbricht reported to General Fromm, had just been assassinated. Mertz von Quirnheim had already issued the preliminary orders for *Valkyrie*.

Fromm was horrified. He snatched up his telephone and placed an emergency call through to the Wolf's Lair. Despite Fellgiebel's efforts, the communication lines from Berlin to East Prussia still functioned. Fromm spoke with Keitel.

> *Fromm.* What's going on in headquarters? Here in Berlin the most incredible rumors are circulating.
> *Keitel.* What do you think's going on? Everything is in order.
> *Fromm.* I've just been told that the Führer has been assassinated!
> *Keitel.* Nonsense! There was an assassination attempt, but it failed. The Führer wasn't even hurt. By the way, where is your Chief of Staff, Colonel Stauffenberg?
> *Fromm.* Stauffenberg hasn't returned yet.[25]

Fromm demanded that Olbricht cancel *Valkyrie* and arrest Mertz. Olbricht left. He instructed the communications people to continue issuing *Valkyrie*.

Stauffenberg and Haeften arrived at Bendlerstrasse just as the *Valkyrie* orders went out. Stauffenberg hastily conferred with Olbricht, Mertz, and others, and together they rushed to Fromm's office.

Olbricht reported to Fromm that Stauffenberg had just confirmed Hitler's death.

"That's impossible," Fromm retorted. "I've just spoken with Keitel! He says the Führer is alive!"

"Keitel's lying as always," Stauffenberg replied. "I was there myself. Hitler is dead."

Given the situation, Olbricht continued, "We have begun Operation *Valkyrie*."

"What do you mean 'we'?" Fromm shouted. "This is mutiny!"

"Sir," Stauffenberg replied heatedly, "I planted the bomb myself . . . nobody could have come out alive."

Fromm, shocked, frantically shouted that Stauffenberg had no other choice, he would have to shoot himself. Stauffenberg interrupted that he had no intention of doing any such thing.

"Then you're all under arrest!" Fromm bellowed.

"Sir," Olbricht said, "you misunderstand the situation here. It is you who are under arrest."[26] Prodded by Mertz's and Haeften's pistols, Fromm retreated to his inner office.

Valkyrie was now underway.

Stauffenberg, over the next few hours, was everywhere. He was constantly on the telephone, reassuring confused and frightened commanders who had just received their *Valkyrie* orders. Hans Bernd Gisevius, who was next to Stauffenberg most of that evening, remembered snatches of Stauffenberg's conversations:

> Keitel's lying. . . . Don't believe him. . . . Hitler is dead. . . . Yes, the operation is underway. . . . I can count on you, can't I? . . . We have to see it through.[27]

Ponderously, *Valkyrie* began to move. Berlin's military commandant, General Paul von Hase, also a conspirator, ordered troops to secure the city center. Count Wolf von Helldorf, Berlin's chief of police and another conspirator, directed his officers to cooperate with the soldiers. Conspirators from all over the city descended on the Bendlerstrasse. There was old General Ludwig Beck, officially the new president, dressed in a business suit to demonstrate that this was not merely a military coup; Eugen Gerstenmaier and Peter Yorck, young intellectuals associated with the Kreisau Circle; Hans Bernd Gisevius, the conspiracy's link to Allen Dulles and Allied Intelligence in Switzerland; Berthold von Stauffenberg, and many others.

Troops entered Berlin. The Berlin Guards Regiment, commanded by a young major named Otto Ernst Remer, deployed long the Wilhelmstrasse and around the Brandenburg Gate and the Tiergarten. In Paris and Vienna and towns throughout Germany, *Valkyrie* came alive.

For a moment, World War II almost ended, and the concentration camps almost closed. But only for a moment for *Valkyrie* began to die almost as soon as it was born.

Hitler's death would have created the hours or even days of confusion which would have permitted a military takeover. But Hitler was not dead, and the Wolf's Lair continued to function. Even as the *Valkyrie* orders went out, the Wolf's Lair rushed out orders countermanding them. By 6:45 P.M., the Deutschlandsender, the National Radio Service, was reporting the assassination attempt, and Hitler's survival.

Out in the army commands, officers were bewildered and frightened. If they disobeyed their *Valkyrie* orders, and the conspirators won, their disobedience might cost them their lives. But if Hitler had indeed survived, and if he prevailed, anyone associated with the conspiracy against him would surely pay with his life. In panic, confusion, and fear, soldiers who had never dreamed of ever being in such a situation had to make up their minds.

Most decided that the safest course would be to wait, to delay, to hesitate, to protect themselves. In response to Stauffenberg's call for valor, most officers chose discretion.

In Berlin, Otto Ernst Remer deployed his soldiers around the city center as ordered, but he was frightened. He was not part of the conspiracy, and the conspirators had had no time to replace him with a confidante. They had gambled that Remer would follow his orders. They lost.

Remer, in his confusion, spoke with his political officer, Hans Hagan. Hagan had friends in Joseph Goebbels's Propaganda Ministry; he told Remer to wait until Hagan spoke with his friends. Hagan rushed to the Propaganda Ministry, only a few blocks from Bendlerstrasse. He was quickly ushered into Goebbels's own office.

Some sort of coup was underway, Goebbels explained excitedly. No one was really sure what was happening, but it seemed like traitors were loose in the city. Goebbels told Hagan to fetch Remer.

Within half an hour, Remer was in Goebbels's office. Goebbels rushed through an emergency call to the Wolf's Lair, and passed the telephone receiver to Remer.

"Do you recognize my voice?" A deep, raspy baritone asked.

"Of course, my Führer!" Remer responded.

"Major Remer," Hitler continued, "a little clique of traitorous and dishonorable officers tried to kill me. But it didn't work. . . . I order you to crush this putsch!"[28]

For a mere major, this was a heady experience. Remer promised his loyalty, and hurried back to his troops. And with that, the coup and the conspirators were doomed.

It was around 7:00 P.M.

In the Bendlerstrasse, Stauffenberg, Olbricht, Mertz von Quirnheim, Haeften, and the others were still making frantic calls, and young officers hurried to and fro with messages and reports.

Ludwig Beck, however, was almost preternaturally calm. He was a professional soldier, the former chief of the General Staff. In 1938, he had resigned in protest, and since then had been at the center of the conspiracy against Hitler. Now, Beck was to be Germany's new president. He was recovering from a cancer operation; always thin, he looked cadaverous. Stoic self-control had always been one of his virtues, and that night, amidst the frantic action, Beck seemed an island of calm. His sangfroid seemed inexplicable to Hans Bernd Gisevius, but Beck quietly explained that once a battle had begun, a commander must keep his head and leave the fighting to his officers.[29]

Only twice did Beck lose his temper. Early in the evening, the commander of the Berlin Military District, General Joachim von Kortzfleish, had rushed to the Bendlerstrasse. His troops were vital to the success of the coup, but *Valkyrie* had terrified Kortz-fleisch.

Beck had calmly explained that, yes, a coup was underway. Shocked, Kortzfleisch stuttered something about "honor" and loyalty to Hitler, and Beck exploded. One could not talk about honor and Hitler in the same breath! Beck ordered Kortzfleisch, weeping and pleading, to be locked up with Fromm.[30]

Later, old Erwin von Witzleben, acerbic and sarcastic, arrived, dressed in his field marshal's uniform. According to the *Valkyrie* orders, Witzleben was to be the new commander-in-chief of the armed forces. Witzleben had been plotting against Hitler since 1938; he and Beck were old comrades. Witzleben had secretly presigned many of the *Valkyrie* orders.

But that night, Witzleben was furious. Where were the troops? There were scarcely any around the Bendlerstrasse, and they seemed to be withdrawing from Berlin. Why were the Nazis still in control of the radio? And why wasn't Hitler dead? In Fromm's office, Beck and Witzleben roared at each other. Beck shouted that the coup couldn't wait. Someone finally had to act! The whole thing was a shambles, Witzleben responded that he was going home, and that he would wait to be arrested there.[31]

It was about 9:00 P.M.

In the humid summer night, the mood in the Bendlerstrasse darkened. Everyone knew what was happening now, everyone knew that the führer was not dead. Soldiers slipped out of doors into the darkness; officers argued in the corridors. Friedrich Olbricht spoke briefly with his son-in-law:

> We had to act, one way or the other. I know what the consequences will be for Eve [Olbricht's wife], Rosemarie [Olbricht's daughter], for your children and you. Nevertheless, for me, the situation is clear. I am a soldier. I am not afraid to die. . . . We'll be able to hold out for a while. Maybe for a night . . . or . . . maybe we'll fall in an hour. . . .

I'm dying for a good cause, of that, I'm absolutely convinced. I'm not doing anything more than thousands of other officers . . . have already done in this war, I'm dying for Germany. I won't die alone, there are many of us here. But there is no other way. Stauffenberg led the charge; we couldn't abandon him.[32]

And then, in the darkening corridors of Bendlerstrasse, there were shouts and curses and finally gunshots. Officers still loyal to Hitler attacked the conspirators. Stauffenberg, wounded, tried to return fire, but was driven down the corridor to Fromm's office. Soon many of them were cornered there, Stauffenberg, Beck, Olbricht, Mertz, Haeften, and others. The shooting stopped, and it was all but over.

General Fromm, surrounded by a cloud of gun-wielding officers, strode into his office. "So, gentlemen," he gloated, "now I will treat you the way you treated me!" If the conspirators had any last personal messages, they had better write them now, Fromm announced, since he would convene a drum-head court-martial immediately. Fromm spun on his heel and left the room, leaving his men to guard the conspirators.

The court-martial took place only a few minutes later. Fromm announced that Olbricht, Mertz, Haeften, and, indicating Stauffenberg, "an officer whose name I refuse to speak," were to be shot immediately. Beck would be spared the indignity of a firing squad. He would be permitted to commit suicide.

Fromm was in a hurry. He handed Beck a pistol. Beck seemed calm, almost bemused. "I'm thinking of earlier times," he murmured. Fromm told him to get on with it.

Beck held the pistol to his head, but at a slight angle. The pistol barked, but the shot only wounded him. He fired again after a moment, and the bullet crashed into his brain.

Guards hustled Stauffenberg, Olbricht, Mertz, and Haeften out into Bendlerstrasse's courtyard, eerily illuminated by truck headlights. The guards pinned white targets to the men's chests. One by one, they stepped before a mound of dirt left by construction workers, and the firing squad killed them.

Stauffenberg shouted something as the bullets struck him. Some thought it sounded like "Long live Germany!"

Fromm made a hoarse speech to the soldiers, called for a "Sieg Heil," and rushed back to his office. Beck's body was on the floor, covered with blood, but incredibly, the old man's heart continued to beat. Fromm pointed at Beck and shouted for someone to kill him. A soldier dragged the body into a corridor and fired into it. Beck's heart stopped.[33]

Bendlerstrasse was swarming now with soldiers and SS troops. Soldiers piled the corpses of Beck, Stauffenberg, Mertz, Olbricht, and Haeften into the back of a truck, and drove off in the darkness to a nearby cemetery. The bodies were tumbled into a common grave and buried.

There was nothing left to do but round up the remaining conspirators like Fritz von der Schulenburg, Ulrich Schwerin von Schwanenfeld, Berthold von Stauffenberg, Peter Yorck von Wartenburg, Eugen Gerstenmaier, and others. Gerstenmaier, a thirty-seven-year-old Protestant theologian and member of Helmut James von Moltke's Kreisau Circle, remembered later:

> When we, a small group of last men, were waiting . . . for the last assault of the advancing SS units, knowing full well that this last attempt of the Germans to help themselves had failed, I heard neither Stauffenberg nor anyone else complain. We had tried to do what we thought we owed Germany and the world before God and our conscience; we had done it with the means which we were able to get hold of, after careful planning and endless efforts. The rest was in God's hands. "In the end, one can do no more than die for the cause," said Ulrich Wilhem Count Schwerin-Schwanenfeld, as we were overpowered, handcuffed to each other, and led away.[34]

It was around midnight.

Meanwhile, Germans huddled near their radios. The Deutschlandsender broadcast a special address by the führer:

> German comrades! Once again, I don't know how many times it has been now, an attempt has been made on my life. I speak to you tonight for two reasons. First, so that you can hear my voice, and know that I am all right, and second, so that you can learn more about a crime without parallel in German history.
>
> A small clique of ambitious, conscienceless . . . stupid officers have hatched a plot to eliminate me and exterminate the leadership of the Armed Forces. Their bomb, planted by Colonel von Stauffenberg, exploded two meters to my right. A number of my close colleagues were injured, one has died. Except for a few bruises and burns, I was completely untouched.
>
> I see in this the hand of Providence, directing me to complete my work. . . .
>
> Now, at a time when the German Armed Forces are engaged in a life and death struggle, a tiny gang appears . . . and tries to stab the nation in the back . . . this gang has nothing to do with the army or

the Armed Forces. It is a gang of criminals, which will be ruthlessly exterminated.[35]

The first act of vengeance occurred just before dawn on Friday, 21 July. SS Chief Heinrich Himmler began to fret about the conspirators' grave. It might become some sort of subversive shrine. Even in death, the conspirators might make trouble. Himmler ordered the SS to send troops to exhume the bodies of Beck, Stauffenberg, Mertz, Haeften, and Olbricht, and destroy them.

SS soldiers returned to the cemetery in the dawn twilight, opened the grave they had just closed, and pulled out the bodies. They drenched the bodies with gasoline and set them on fire. When the flames died out, they scattered the ashes and the bones.[36]

2

Vermächtnis

It's true: you're innocent. I, too, born almost late enough, am
held to be free from guilt. Only if I wanted to forget, if you
were unwilling to learn how it slowly happened, only then
might words of one syllable catch up with us: words like guilt
and shame; they, too, resolute snails, impossible to stop.
— Günter Grass, *From the Diary of a Snail*

"So," Fritz von der Schulenburg remarked on the night of 20 July
1944, "it seems that the German people must drain this cup to
the dregs. We must sacrifice ourselves. But posterity will justify
us."[1] In one of his last letters, written just before his execution,
Schulenburg expressed the same confident hope: "What we did
was insufficient, but, in the end, history will judge and acquit us.
You know that I was inspired by patriotism."[2] General Friedrich
Olbricht thought about posterity too on the night of 20 July. One
of the coup's survivors remembered that Olbricht said:

> I do not know how posterity will judge our actions and myself. But
> I know with certainty that we have acted without personal motive,
> and only risked all in a desperate situation to save Germany from
> complete ruin. I am convinced that posterity will one day recognize
> and understand this.[3]

Fritz Schulenburg and Friedrich Olbricht were wrong. Posterity has neither completely approved nor entirely understood.

Posterity has idealized the conspiracy and condemned it; sanctified the conspirators and vilified them. Posterity has brooded
over the conspiracy; as of 1984, the fortieth anniversary of the
conspiracy, some six thousand publications had been devoted to
the German anti-Nazi resistance, and many of these dealt in one
way or another with the 20 July plot.[4] Posterity has fretted over
and gnawed at and broken its teeth on the conspiracy,[5] and re-

38

fused to let it go. The conspiracy's "Vermächtnis." Its "legacy" has been in probate now for nearly five decades, and its heirs show little sign of compromise.[6]

"Ah, now, really, gentlemen, this is a little late," Friedrich Reck-Malleczewin wrote bitterly in his diary the day after the coup. No one was closer ideologically or socially to the conspirators than this Prussian aristocrat, murdered by the Nazis in 1945, and no one more angrily condemned the conspiracy.

> You made this monster, and so long as things were going well you gave him whatever he wanted. You turned Germany over to this arch-criminal, you swore allegiance to him. . . . I am a conservative. . . . I was brought up as a monarchist . . . and yet . . . I hate you. . . .
>
> The nation mourns the fact that bomb did not explode where and when it should have. . . . But as to the generals: as soon as Germany is liberated . . . they should be killed, along with the industrialists who launched this war . . . and, let us not forget, the whole crew responsible for the immense misdeed of January 30, 1933, who ought to be hanged twenty feet higher than the rest. . . .
>
> I can't help it.[7]

Otto John, one of the civilians involved in the conspiracy, succeeded in his desperate escape from Berlin, and by mid-July 1944, he had made it to Madrid. He contacted an old friend, Don Luis Ruiz de Valdivia, and explained to him what he and the conspirators had tried to do. Valdivia, a gruff old man, was unimpressed. His only comment was: "Wrong, and too late."[8]

The western allies were just as hostile. In its editorial of 9 August 1944, for example, the New York Times dismissed the assassination attempt as a "gangster" affair, proof that German officers were no better than their odious leader.[9] In an editorial entitled "International Swine," the New York Herald Tribune commented:

> Americans as a whole will not feel sorry that the bomb spared Hitler for liquidation of his generals. They hold no brief for aristocrats as such, especially those given to the goosestep, and, when it connives with their convenience, to collaboration with low-born, mob-rousing corporals. Let the generals kill the corporal, or vice-versa, preferably both.[10]

Some Communist resisters in 1945 had similar feelings. Fritz Selbmann, a Communist resister imprisoned in the Flossenberg concentration camp, remembered later:

We learned about the July 1944 attempt on Hitler's life long after it occurred, and our information was fragmentary. Naturally, we were happy to hear about the conspiracy against Hitler, led by men belonging to circles closest to the Nazis. We cursed the plot's failure. Then I heard that Carl Goerdeler was the conspiracy's leader. I had known Goerdeler from my days in Leipzig. He had been mayor, and was the archetypical ultra-reactionary bureaucrat. I knew then that the only thing lost in the failed conspiracy were the lives of a few good men, who had sacrificed themselves for a doubtful cause.[11]

The political left, at first though, embraced the conspirators. Anton Ackermann, a spokesman for the Communist Free Germany National Committee, said in a Moscow radio broadcast on 21 July 1944: "We don't know who the men were who acted against Hitler, nor do we ask. Whoever fights against Hitler . . . deserves the active support of all decent Germans."[12] Two days later, an editorial signed by the National Committee's leadership, proclaimed: "Every blow struck against Hitler, no matter by whom, is a strike against the archenemy of our country. Every act against Hitler and his agents is a truly patriotic deed."[13]

The conspiracy's first students, such as Hans Rothfels and Allen Dulles, argued that the conspirators were brave men and patriots.[14] Countess Marion Dönhoff, in a 1945 essay, agreed. In the midst of all the horrors committed in Germany's name during the war, she wrote, the effort of the July 20 Conspirators to assassinate Hitler and end the war was noble. Their epitaph, Dönhoff concluded, should be the lines from 1 Maccabees 9: "If our time to die has come / We will die well / For our brothers / and to preserve our honor."[15]

Opinions changed. By the tenth anniversary of the plot, the Western Allies, and especially the West Germans, had translated the July 20 Conspiracy into a political icon, and the conspirators into saints. For conservative Germans especially, the 20 July plot provided a way to be both traditionally patriotic and simultaneously anti-Nazi. As Kurt Tauber notes in his history of postwar German nationalism:

In the postwar years, the Twentieth of July has been more than just the date when an inadequately prepared coup failed to remove the dictator and to prevent thereby the country's ultimate disintegration. The Twentieth of July has provided the moral justification for the Bonn Republic, the password which has enabled Germany to re-enter the larger republic of common decency.[16]

The conspiracy provided an ideological foundation for the "Bundeswehr," the West German Army, writes Claus Donate.

"The military is the key to the resistance," is the fundamental thesis which appears in all the Bundeswehr texts. The symbol of the resistance, and often the only act of resistance described, is July 20th, which was led "primarily by soldiers," most of them, the texts continue, "aristocrats."[17]

The West German government in the 1950s began to publish a variety of materials about the conspiracy. Streets, plazas, and army barracks were named after Claus von Stauffenberg, Ludwig Beck, and other conspirators. Even people only marginally involved with the plot, such as Field Marshal Erwin Rommel, were sanctified by their association with it. Berlin's Plötzensee prison, where many of the conspirators were executed, became a national shrine, and West German teachers, especially in the 1950s, typically taught their pupils that anti-Nazi resistance meant the 20 July plot. Other forms of German resistance, that, for example, of women, workers, adolescents, Jews, and especially the political left, was largely ignored.[18] Foundations such as Munich's Institut für Zeitgeschichte (Institute for Contemporary History), and the Forschungsgemeinschaft 20. Juli (July 20th Research Group), devoted great energy to preserving the memory of the July 20 Conspirators.

Still, West German enthusiasm for the conspiracy was not unanimous. A June 1951 opinion poll asked West Germans: "In your opinion, how are the men of July 20th to be judged?" The response was:

40 percent approved the actions of the conspirators
30 percent condemned the conspirators
16 percent refused to comment
11 percent had never heard of the conspiracy
 3 percent gave ambiguous answers

According to a November 1952 poll, some 36 percent of West Germans questioned believed that German resistance to Hitler was responsible for Germany's defeat.[19]

West Germany's cranky neo-Nazi groups claimed that the conspirators were nothing but traitors. Otto Ernst Remer, the man most immediately responsible for the conspiracy's destruction, spent the 1950s vilifying the conspirators. Remer argued that

they were responsible for German defeats in France; they sabo-
taged the war effort on the Eastern Front; and, Remer later wrote,
praise for the conspiracy was responsible, in the 1960s and
1970s, for "anarchists, terrorists, Marxists [and] mobs in the
streets."[20] It is simply inconceivable, Remer insists, "that any
other civilized nation would defend, not to mention honor, men
who betrayed their country."[21] Hans Hagen, Remer's ally in sup-
pressing the coup in July 1944, added that the reason the plot
failed was the conspirators' cowardice. "How is it that Adolf Hitler survived?" Hagen asks. Because among the conspirators
"there was no spirit of self-sacrifice."[22]

East German historians, meanwhile, divided the July 20 Conspirators into relatively "progressive" groups such as the "Stauffenberg group," and "reactionaries" such as the "Goerdeler
group." As Klaus Finker argues in his biography of Stauffenberg:

> Clearly, the conspiracy was, overall a reactionary enterprise, in-
> tended to save German imperialism and the power of monopoly capi-
> tal from destruction. It is unscientific dilletantism to speak of the
> conspiracy as a "rebellion of conscience," or an expression of the
> "spirit of freedom," or as a democratic conspiracy against totalitar-
> ianism. To be sure, the group around [Helmut James] Moltke, [Julius]
> Leber, and [Claus] Stauffenberg represented bourgeois-democratic
> patriotic tendencies—but this group stood in contradiction to the
> conspiracy in general.[23]

By the plot's twentieth and thirtieth anniversaries, Western
historians were also becoming increasingly uneasy with the "legend" of 20 July.[24] An inevitable "gerontophagy"[25] began, as
younger historians attacked the "mythologies" of their elders.

Hannah Arendt had quite early dismissed praise of the conspiracy as an "alibi."[26] Martin Niemoeller was a conservative
leader of the anti-Nazi movement in the German Protestant
church. He was sent to the Dachau concentration camp because
of his resistance. Niemoeller was close ideologically and personally to some of the conspirators, yet he nevertheless wrote in
1967: "Those of us in Dachau learned quickly about the July
20th events . . . at that time, I was convinced that, had I been free,
I would have participated in the conspiracy. Today, given my
spiritual development since then, I am convinced that participation in the plot would be impossible for me."[27]

The plot's acceptance of assassination, and above all its politi-
cally conservative tone, made it impossible for the older Niemoeller to endorse it. Ralf Dahrendorf, a liberal political scientist

and scholar, spoke of the Plot as a "revolt of tradition, and thus of the illiberalism and of the authoritarianism of a surviving past,"[28] and Hermann Graml, Hans Mommson, and their colleagues have outlined in detail the antidemocratic, nationalist, and often imperialist values of especially the older members of the conspiracy.[29] Klaus-Jürgen Müller, an expert on the life of Ludwig Beck, criticized the "moralizing" tone of much of the literature on the conspiracy.[30] While some students of the conspiracy continued to agree with Hans Rothfels that the 20 July Conspiracy laid the foundations for a democratic Germany, many others, by the 1960s and 1970s, disagreed. "The German resistance cannot . . . be understood as the hour of birth of post-war Germany," writes Karl Otmar von Aretin; "a straight line from the resistance to our democracy cannot be drawn," argue the editors of the Bibliographie "Widerstand."[31] Younger historians, trained in social history and suspicious of the conservative agenda often concealed in the 20 July hagiography, have expanded the concept of resistance to include a wide variety of nonconformist behavior, have focused their attention on previously ignored forms of resistance, and prefer the language of sociological analysis to discourse rooted in the archaic, and, to them, suspect, vocabulary of "conscience" and "virtue."[32]

Time, meanwhile, took its toll on memory. In 1970, some 49 percent of young West Germans (ages 16–29) could correctly identify the significance of the date "20 July." By 1984, only 33 percent of people in the same age group could; in fact, 42 percent of West Germans questioned knew little or nothing about 20 July.[33]

Although time may have blurred the memory of 20 July, it did not blunt the bitterness of some who remembered. For example, 1978 was a very difficult year for West Germans. The previous year had witnessed the worst of West German terrorism. Revelations in 1977 and 1978 that the conservative minister-president of Baden-Württemberg, Hans Filbinger, had, as a Navy lawyer, and contrary to his repeated denials, condemned sailors to death in the last months of the war, provoked an angry national debate. The Düsseldorf trial of the Majdenek concentration camp guards resurrected all the guilt, and the flight from guilt, associated with the war's horrors. A new book by David Irving seemed to prove that Field Marshal Erwin Rommel was not the anti-Nazi hero West Germans had come to believe; Der Spiegel, West Germany's leading news magazine, entitled its cover story, which reviewed Irving's book, "Field Marshal Rommel: End of a Legend."[34]

In 1978, as a gesture of national reconciliation, the 20 July
Research Group invited Herbert Wehner, the Social Democratic
party's Parliamentary leader, to give the memorial address at
services commemorating the thirty-fourth anniversary of the
coup. The 20 July Research Group hoped that in this troubled
time, the memory of the plot could reunite the nation. Wehner
had been in the Communist resistance during the war. His
speech, honoring the primarily conservative resisters, could
bring the nation together.

It didn't. Franz Ludwig Graf Schenk von Stauffenberg, Claus
Stauffenberg's son and a conservative member of Parliament, angrily objected to Wehner's proposed speech. His father, Stauffenberg claimed, and not died for communism. It was outrageous
that Wehner, the former Communist, was to be the keynote
speaker at the 20 July memorial.

Children of other conspirators immediately attacked Stauffenberg. Their fathers, they argued, had tried to forge an anti-Nazi
alliance that included, not excluded, the political left.

All of these arguments, carried on in the media, soured the
memorial. In the end, neither Wehner nor Stauffenberg participated in the 1978 services.[35] At the same time, a group calling
itself the "Society for an Open Media" launched a bitter attack
on the conspirators at its 1978 convention. The conspirators, the
Society announced, had "stabbed the nation in the back".[36]

Meanwhile, the 20 July 1978 edition of East Germany's official
newspaper, Neues Deutschland, ignored the anniversary of the
conspiracy entirely, but devoted lengthy articles to the Filbinger
Affair, the Majdenek trial, and West German neo-Nazi groups.[37]

In 1984, the World War II allies celebrated the fortieth anniversary of Europe's liberation from Nazism. The Soviets and "their"
Germans jointly conducted ceremonies in the East. The Western
Allies held memorial services at Normandy and elsewhere, but
did not invite "their" Germans to attend. West German Chancellor Helmut Kohl responded by recalling the memory of German
anti-Nazis, particularly the men of 20 July. They too, Kohl insisted, had died for freedom and human rights.

Kohl's claim infuriated some observers. The American journal,
The New Republic, for example, in an editorial entitled "Misplaced Gratitude," retorted:

The conspirators suffered a terrible death, and some of them did
indeed demonstrate courage. . . . [But] the conspiracy was not inspired by a special concern for "human rights and freedom" or for

"justice and truth" . . . these conspirators were right-wing patriots; they—and Count von Stauffenberg in particular—were motivated by the impending defeat of the Fatherland, which was inevitable after Normandy. . . . They were not at all moved by what Hitler, the conspirators themselves, and the German people had done to millions of innocents.[38]

President Ronald Reagan's maladroit attempt, in 1985, to ease bruised West German feelings by visiting a German military cemetery that included SS graves, only triggered in Germany and elsewhere another round of recriminations and accusations.[39]

On the tenth anniversary of the coup, in 1954, Theodor Heuss, West Germany's first president, proclaimed during a memorial service at Berlin's Free University: "The German soul is moved to thanksgiving, thanksgiving for the inheritance ('vermächtnis') it has received—these brave deaths sacrificed for the life of the nation."[40] But as journalist Ralph Giordano pointed out in 1987, this inheritance is painful and ambiguous. Any discussion of 20 July entangles one in Germany's "second guilt." The "first guilt" is the direct guilt for the horrors of the Second World War. The "second guilt" arises from Germany's troubled and painful effort to come to terms with the first guilt. The 20 July Conspirators— they were heroes, but they were also traitors. They did try to destroy Nazism, but Nazism might never had lasted as long as it did without their complicity. They were good people, and brave, but their hands were dirty. The West German government constantly praised the conspirators, but at the same time proved reluctant to condemn the people who had crushed the conspiracy. For years, German courts struggled with suit and countersuit regarding former Nazi officials who had destroyed the plot and killed the plotters. Yes, the courts seemed to say, the conspirators were right. But yes, too, they said at the same time that the Nazi officials were justified as well, since after all the conspirators were committing treason. Which is not to say, to be sure, that the conspirators were actually traitors. . . . Out of this confusion arises the "second guilt," the "burden" of being German; few topics trigger this second guilt, this burden, more immediately than 20 July. According to Giordano, historian Jörg Friedrich explains the situation well. In Friedrich's words:

The resisters were never fully accepted, their executioners never entirely condemned. The Hitler system was neither completely annulled, nor completely accepted. . . . The Federal Republic tried to please everyone. It was the Fatherland of Nazi Party members as

well as those the Nazis called "enemies of the people," the denounced and the neutral, the persecuted and their persecutors.[41]

Decades later, 20 July remains disturbing and dangerous.

For nearly a half-century now, 20 July has perplexed and fascinated posterity. Why this troubled fascination with a failed coup?

Partly, of course, it is all politics. As the conspiracy evolved
into a right-wing icon, it attracted left-wing iconoclasts. The
1978 fight over Herbert Wehner's 20 July speech, for example,
had far more to do with 1978 partisan politics than with the
1944 plot.

Mostly, though, it is the event itself that attracts and provokes
because of its drama. It is dramatic, of course, in a superficial way,
what with its smuggled bombs, shadowy rendezvous, sudden
escapes, and bursts of violence. But 20 July is dramatic in a far
more profound way. It probes, like all drama, to the essence of
things, to the soul and to the conscience, and this is the source
of its fascination—the reason why it deserves to be revisited
again and again.

The conspirators themselves were struck by the dramatic quality of their experience. Ulrich von Hassell, a professional diplomat and conspirator, cited the famous lines from Shakespeare's
Henry V, "We few, we happy few, we band of brothers" to describe
the conspirators.[42] Hans Bernd von Haeften, a foreign service
officer, and, like his brother, Werner, a conspirator, used a modified line from Goethe as his motto. In Goethe's play, *Götz von
Berlichingen*, a character says: "The evil will rule, and with
treachery will snare the good in their nets." Haeften often remarked that "the time must come when the good will conspire
and snare the evil in their nets."[43] Theo Haubach, a social-demo-
cratic journalist and member of the anti-Nazi Kreisau Circle,
wrote in 1939: "The task that falls to us is like the tragic conflict
of the classical drama. Hitler must be destroyed and, at the same
time, the German people must be saved from disaster. How can
we few, with an eye to reality, bring this about?"[44]

And in his unfinished *Ethics*, Dietrich Bonhoeffer brooded:

> . . . our period, more than any earlier period in the history of the
> West, is oppressed by a superabounding reality of concrete ethical
> problems. . . . Today there are once more villains and saints, and they

are not hidden from public view. . . . Shakespeare's characters walk
in our midst. . . . They emerge from primeval depths and by their
appearance they tear open the infernal or divine abyss from which
they come and enable us to see for a moment into mysteries of which
we had never dreamed.[45]

3

Charakter

A man's moral worth is sure only at the point where he is prepared to give his life for his convictions.
                                        —Henning von Tresckow

On 11 April 1943, General Henning von Tresckow's two sons were confirmed in the Lutheran church. The ceremony took place in Potsdam's Garrison Church, the old chapel hallowed in Prussian tradition. Almost exactly a decade before, Chancellor Adolf Hitler had opened his first Parliament there. Hitler wore a frock-coat for the occasion instead of his brown uniform, showed every respect for the ancient president, Field Marshal Paul von Hindenburg, invoked all the good old virtues in his address, and convinced his conservative audience that he really was a traditionalist at heart—something, to be sure, they wanted to believe anyway. That was in March 1933. The Tresckow service, almost exactly ten years later, was a more modest affair. There was a war on and General von Tresckow was home only briefly; he was on leave from the Russian Front.

Henning von Tresckow, forty-two years old that spring, was a professional soldier. He had served as a young officer in the Great War, and had briefly left the army in the 1920s to work as a banker. Though military promotions in the 1920s were slow, and an officer's pay not quite that of a banker's, Tresckow abandoned his bank and returned to the army. He attended the War College in the mid-1930s, and was appointed to the General Staff. Cool, efficient, reserved, his thinning hair closely cropped, his bearing athletic, Tresckow was the model staff officer. Like Claus von Stauffenberg, Tresckow was one of the bright young men on the General Staff when the war began.

At the confirmation service, General von Tresckow made a little speech. "Never forget," he told his sons,

48

. . . that you have grown up on Prussian soil, with Prussian-German
values, and that today, you have been confirmed in the holiest shrine
of old Prussia. This brings with it great responsibilities—the responsibility to tell the truth, to be disciplined, to do your duty always.
But you should never think that this exhausts Prussian values. Often
Prussianness is misunderstood. Freedom can never be divorced from
real Prussian values. Real Prussianness is a synthesis of commitment
and freedom, of subordination and command, of pride in yourself
and understanding for others, of firmness and compassion. Without
this synthesis, there is a danger of sinking into a soulless bureaucracy
and arrogance. Only in this synthesis can be found the German and
European task of Prussia, the "prussian dream."[1]

Tresckow's talk, with its mixture of patriotism and piety, might
seem simply the kind of thing a German general would inevitably
say at his sons' confirmation. In retrospect, the sermon was remarkable. For the general delivering it was an assassin.

They are hard men to understand, these "frondeurs." What
were they like? Their images are preserved in the old black and
white photographs, their faces inevitably sober and severe, but
what were they like? How did their voices sound; what gestures
did they make; what were their habits, their fears, their faults,
their joys? The question is of central importance, for without
knowing something about their character, one can hardly discuss
their moral imagination. From letters and diaries, from bits of
remembered conversations, it is possible to construct, cautiously
and tentatively, a kind of group portrait. The evidence is fragmentary and impressionistic to be sure, the portrait is at best sugges-
tive rather than definitive, a sketch at most. Still, with care, it
can be made; from shadows and murmurs, their image can still
be evoked.

If asked to describe themselves, what would the conspirators
say?
Not much. They would undoubtedly find the question imperti-
nent. Democratic friendliness was not one of the conspirators'
charms. They were a stiff, cool, distant bunch. Marion Yorck von
Wartenburg, Peter's widow, wrote rather wistfully years later
about her generation: "We were raised differently in those days.
We never gave our emotions free rein. Still, I don't think our
education in self-restraint did us any harm."[2] Of her husband,
who, with Helmuth James von Moltke, was one of the founders
of the Kreisau Circle, Marion Yorck wrote: "He never really was

able to be open and natural. He was rather closed, and reserved, although always courteous."[3]

Dietrich Bonhoeffer walked with "very straight knees, which made his gait look taut, almost rigid."[4] One of Bonhoeffer's students remembered, "He liked to keep his distance, and he did not permit any undue familiarity."[5] Another student commented about Bonhoeffer: "He was by nature reserved. I was astonished when he told me that beside his relatives, he only called one person 'du.'"[6] Another acquaintance remembered that "in the lecture room, Bonhoeffer was very concentrated, quite unsentimental, almost dispassionate, clear as crystal, with a certain rational coldness . . . [he] was always an outsider."[7] According to Eberhard Bethge, Bonhoeffer's student, friend, relative (Bethge married Bonhoeffer's niece), and biographer: "Just as he never approached too near to anyone, he never let anyone get too near to him; for that reason, some people found him rather proud . . . the more intense his emotions, the more he cloaked them in simple words and gestures."[8]

Once, Bonhoeffer was returning with friends from a conference. They hurried to their train station only to discover that their train was on the opposite track. His friends ignored the warning signs and bounded across the tracks; Bonhoeffer insisted on following the walkway the railroad signs designated. One of his companions later wrote: "The smallest offense against order shocked him. For the sake of the order which had been destroyed on a grand scale, he became a revolutionary."[9] "Discipline" ("Zucht") was one of Bonhoeffer's favorite words.[10]

About Helmuth James von Moltke, Michael Balfour, who knew him well, said:

> . . . self-restraint fitted in with his dark clothes, plain white shirt, and habitual black tie. In spite of all his zest for life, he had an austere side corresponding to the melancholy strain in his character which sometimes made him critical of those whom he thought over-indulgent.[11]

And a friend wrote of Berthold von Stauffenberg:

> His nature was exclusive, though not in a social sense. He knew the rules of society, although he didn't always seem to follow them. There was always something awkward about him, he was like some good-hearted, shy young boy. . . . Many people gave up trying to get near him, because he really wasn't very good at small talk. . . . He was more eccentric than conventional. . . . He loved the visual arts and

music, but he lived for poetry, for there was the soil in which he was rooted.[12]

They were cool and also ironic characters, possessing what a dramatist might describe as a kind of "histrionic sensibility," a "habit of significant make-believe."[13] Part actor, part spectator, sure of themselves yet distant from themselves, schooled in a world of intricate social cues, the conspirators slipped in and out of roles easily.

They liked masks. Bonhoeffer cites Nietzsche's comment, "Every profound mind requires a mask," with approval.[14] Fritz von der Schulenburg, with his monocle, dueling scars, and "almost mask-like face and outrageously tough look," easily played the role of the "haughty Junker." When in a heated argument, his favorite gesture to stress a point was to wave a clenched fist beneath his interlocutor's nose. Yet, ferocious as he was, he normally spoke quietly, lived simply, was a nature enthusiast, and wept when he read poetry.[15] Claus von Stauffenberg loved to play the "advocatus diaboli," the "devil's-advocate" in arguments, often making it remarkably difficult to determine what his "real" opinions were.[16] Dietrich Bonhoeffer, an intensely commited Christian and theologian, "never," one who knew him recalled, "took a theological argument with ultimate seriousness."[17]

The conspirators had a kind of ironic imagination that gave them both a charming decorum, a delight in "courtly" and "chivalrous" behavior,[18] as well as a comic panache. Their sobriety and formality made their understated wit and their occasional bits of buffoonery all the more striking. Adam Trott's friends, for example, spoke of his laconic eloquence.[19] Henning von Tresckow was meticulously polite; he added "please" even to his orders to subordinates, and it seemed to some that he was "born to be a 'grand seigneur.'"[20] But friends remembered that in private Tresckow could be quite witty.[21]

Juxtaposed to the conspirators' ritualized formality was an equally elaborate, occasionally foppish, informality. The younger soldiers among the conspirators, for example, were notorious for their rather bohemian costume. Henning von Tresckow, the efficient General Staff officer, disliked uniforms and preferred wearing civilian clothes.[22] A 1933 efficiency report on Claus von Stauffenberg noted this about the young officer:

> ... reliable and independent character ... remarkable intellectual gifts ... superior tactical and technical ability ... quite aware of his

military ability and intellectual superiority, he sometimes tends to a certain arrogance, which expresses itself in sarcasm, which however, is never really wounding. Rather careless in appearance; his manner as a young officer could be a bit crisper.[23]

Fritz von der Schulenburg refused to button his uniform jacket properly, and often dressed in a unique combination of military and mufti. Of an encounter with Schulenburg, an officer later wrote that he was shocked that "this badly brushed and almost negligently dressed young man, totally devoid of military bearing, should be the famous count."[24]

They could be almost vaudevillian at times. In 1937, for instance, when Albrecht Mertz von Quirnheim and Claus von Stauffenberg were young officers attending the War College, they invented as part of a Christmas skit some "tactical aphorisms" to reflect what they had learned about military life; one of them was: "Faith, Hope, and Stupidity, these three abide, but the greatest of these is Stupidity."[25] Six years later, when Stauffenberg was recovering from his severe war wounds, he breakfasted one spring day with Mertz and Rudolf Fahrner, a friend and scholar. They ate outside, had honey for their toast, and suddenly were attacked by a flight of wasps. Fahrner remembered:

> I can still see Claus having breakfast with Mertz von Quirnheim on the balcony in the morning sun. Some wasps were after their honey. . . . They sent Claus running. The one good thing about his injuries, he joked, was that, without worrying about being misrepresented, he could now openly show his fear of wasps. Before that he has always had to conceal it.[26]

Stauffenberg had to conceal it because among the conspirators' families and social mileau, the great sign of good breeding was to respond to any sort of stress with aplomb and understatement. A friend once warned the young diplomat, Adam von Trott zu Solz, for example, that his plotting treason from within the Foreign Office was extraordinarily dangerous. Trott replied that the safest place for a bird to build its nest was "in the scarecrow's pocket."[27] Helmut James von Moltke, according to Balfour,

> . . . was a complicated character. . . . On the one hand he had a decided taste for society, provided it was interesting. . . . Moreover, he liked his company mixed. . . . He has sometimes been described as witty . . . but . . . Mrs. Mowrer is nearer the mark in referring to his "impish" sense of humor. . . . He liked to tease people . . . and had

a keen sense of the ludicrous, the incongruous, and the bogus. To amuse and interest his audience, he tended to present life dramatically. . . . Yet on the other hand, he seldom revealed his inner self or thoughts.[28]

In prison, in the last weeks of his life, a fellow inmate remarked that Moltke must certainly be hoping for a reprieve. Moltke responded cooly, "hoping is not my métier."[29]

The conspirators' ironic cast of mind and chilly reserve might have bred a kind of paralyzing skepticism and caution; to the contrary, however, it seemed to encourage an enthusiasm for action. Indeed, in retrospect, they seem indefatigable. Peter Yorck constantly "yearned for action."[30] Major Karl Freiherr von Thungen, one of Stauffenberg's collegues in Berlin, wrote later:

I never opened Claus's door without seeing him on the telephone. Before him would be a pile of papers, he would hold the telephone receiver in one hand, a pencil in the other, and as he spoke, he would work through the files. He always spoke with enthusiasm, praising . . . or reproving . . . or commanding . . . but always writing at the same time. . . . Next to him would be a secretary, rushing to take the files, and letters, and notes from him. . . . He could work through documents with blinding speed, and his comments were always so precise and to the point that he often threw people reporting to him into confusion.[31]

Dietrich Bonhoeffer was the same way. In April 1934, for instance, he urged the European Christian ecumenical movement to repudiate the Nazified German church. He wrote:

One has to decide. One can't wait forever for a sign from heaven to fall in one's lap and solve all problems . . . to refuse to act from fear of failure . . . seems to me to offend against love. Postponed or avoided decisions can be more sinful that false decisions. "Too late" is the same thing as "never." . . . Someone must fearlessly take the lead.[32]

"Action," Bonhoeffer wrote in his *Ethics*, "is and must continue to be the only possible attitude towards the law of God."[33]

Stauffenberg and Bonhoeffer were, to be sure, young men relatively unencumbered by the experience of age. But even the older members of the conspiracy displayed a distinct "decisionist" quality. Carl Goerdeler, his co-conspirator Joseph Müller quipped, was a kind of "little engine," which, Müller com-

plained, always ran too noisily.[34] Ludwig Beck was often criticized for his caution, yet it was Beck's resignation as Army chief
of staff in 1938 that marks the most dramatic moment of the first
phase of the conservative opposition, and it was his tenacity that
held the conspiracy together during the early 1940s, when Hitler
seemed unbeatable. Once Henning von Tresckow decided in
early 1943 that assassinating Hitler was Germany's only hope,
his resolve was utterly unshakable. And, as Fabian von Schlabrendorff writers, the conspiracy itself, the constant fear of betrayal, the endless frustrations, and the simple need to maintain
a credible "cover" by performing duties that kept in power the
very regime one was secretly opposing was all mentally, morally,
and physically exhausting, and demanded extraordinary re-
serves of energy.[35]

Before the war, all this energy found a host of creative outlets.
Most of the conspirators were multilingual and widely traveled.
Beck was a francophile. Bonhoeffer, Moltke, and Trott all studied
or worked in Britain. Oster, Stauffenberg, and Bonhoeffer were
accomplished amateur musicians. Stauffenberg, the young cavalry officer, was, as a young man, an active member of poet Stephan George's circle of Bohemian aesthetes. Missie
Vassiltchikov's comments about her superior in the Foreign Office, Adam Trott, are representative of those applied to many of
Trott's fellow conspirators. Trott, thirty-five years old in 1944,
had been a Rhodes scholar, and Missie wrote of him in her diary:

> ... he has remarkable eyes ... it is perhaps his intensity which is
> somehow so striking ... he is brilliantly intelligent ... we usually
> speak English together ... when he speaks German he becomes so
> intellectual that I cannot always follow. ... He throws the beginning
> of a sentence into the air, pauses for a second, and the rest comes
> tumbling after.[36]

They seemed almost purposely contrary, self-conscious bun-
dles of contradictions. Karl Barth, the great Swiss theologian,
once remarked that he found in Dietrich Bonhoeffer a certain
uncanny quality; he was always surprised by the new ways Bonhoeffer found to look at things.[37] Manfred von Brauchitsch, who
served with Stauffenberg, remembered him as

> ... a strange, unusual man, far above the average officer. In a "Prus-
> sian" sense he was never a "regular soldier"; with his casual de-
> meanor, he seemed rather unmilitary. ... He enjoyed company, but
> completely rejected the hard-drinking and carousing so common

among his brother officers. . . . Among women, he was shy and very polite, and he disliked the sexual "adventures" his comrades engaged in; indeed, he simply could not understand their behavior.[38]

Yet, as Kurt Bauch recalled, this seemingly shy officer enjoyed enormous prestige among his peers. Stauffenberg, Bauch writes, was:

> . . . a colonel who looked like a poet . . . young, but intensely serious, badly disabled, yet in full control of himself . . . the moment he began to speak in his soft, clipped manner, everyone else fell silent. . . . Despite . . . superhuman strain, he would briefly discuss any caller's affairs with him, in complete composure—and in a few minutes, everything was clear and settled.[39]

Hauteur and eccentricity, ironic detachment and enthusiastic commitment, were not the products of random selection. The conspirators were characters who followed a complex script one part neoclassical, one part orthodox Christian. They had absorbed this code from the humanist gymnasia most attended; from the religiously orthodox families in which most had grown up; and from the canon of literature they inherited, based on Schiller and Goethe. They imbued it from the idealized vision they held of Frederick the Great and the Prussian reformers of the early nineteenth century. This particular blend of values is hardly unique to Germany, yet it was remarkably powerful in Germany.[40] Its grand and paradoxical lesson was that one fullfils one's "self" only by dramatically expanding one's self beyond one's self, and thereby, in a sense, "losing" one's narrow self and gaining a greater self; that life is fullest when it is sacrificed nobly. According to Schiller:

> . . . sacrificing one's life is purposeless, since life is the basis of all good. Yet from a moral point of view, sacrificing one's life is the highest good, since life is never simply for itself, it is itself not a goal, but a means to express moral value.[41]

Later generations might find Schiller's words incomprehensible; eighteenth-century audiences found them noble, and so did the conspirators. In 1933, Adolf Hitler cited Schiller's lines in proclaiming the Third Reich: "We want to be one people of brothers / Undivided by need or danger." In 1944, in the proclamations the conspirators hoped to issue, Claus von Stauffenberg insisted on adding Schiller's next two lines, which Hitler had ignored: "We want to live free, as our fathers did, / Better to die than live in slavery."[42]

The conspirators expressed this cult of self-sacrifice in little things, such as Henning von Tresckow's habit of closing telephone conversations with "bin jederzeit für Sie da"—"I'm always here if you need anything"[43]—and Bonhoeffer's unfailing availability to his students.[44]

They expressed it as well in their enthusiasm for public service. All the conspirators came from families with long traditions of public service, not in electoral politics, but in law, civil service, the ministry, and especially the military. For the conspirators, who they were blended easily with what they did. The sense of division between "real selves" and "occupations" which so plagues moderns was not typical of them. For the conspirators, their "real selves" could be found only through self-restraint, and if necessary, self-sacrifice, in public service. They had, in other words, "callings," not "careers."[45]

Above all, the conspirators' sense of self-restraint in service of the public realm appeared in the ideal of "dying well." Schooled in the aesthetics of self-restraint, convinced of the priority of the public life, the conspirators could think of no nobler demonstration of their values than to cooly sacrifice their lives for the public good. When Friedrich Olbricht remarked to his son-in-law on the night of 20 July that "he was a soldier, he knew how to die," and that he, like so many other soldiers, was "dying for Germany," he was not simply repeating patriotic cant. He was, instead, preparing himself to die well.

Perhaps the gravest moral dilemma the conspirators faced was that this ethic of sacrifice had been hijacked by Hitler. Hitler was remarkably adept at manipulating this ethic for his own ends by convincing people that they indeed ought to die well. The conspirators had to learn, painfully, that dying well was not enough, that what one died for was even more important than how the dying was done.

By 1944, they learned that what one died for could be noble only if it was exemplary. The conspirators shared with other European resisters what James Wilkenson has called a belief in ". . . the spiritual power of exemplary acts."[46] An action's primary value was to be found in its symbolism and its expressiveness, not its utility. It is symbolism, not utility, which ennobles. Ideally, to be sure, a public action will be both symbolically expressive and effective, but effectiveness is of secondary importance, and in extreme cases, the nobility of an action is enhanced by its utter lack of utility.

Early in the summer of 1944, for example, shortly before the coup, Claus von Stauffenberg, through an intermediary, asked Henning von Tresckow whether there was any point any longer in launching the coup. By June 1944, Nazi Germany was clearly doomed—the Western Allies had invaded France, the Russians had launched a crushing offensive in the East, few German officers were willing to support the coup, and the chances of the coup's success were minimal. Under the circustances, was the conspiracy still worth the risk? Was the coup attempt worth the conspirators' lives? Stauffenberg, to be sure, was determined to go ahead with the coup, but he wanted Tresckow's advice.

Tresckow answered: "We must act in Berlin whatever the cost. Even if it is sure to fail, it must be attempted nevertheless. For it is no longer a question of practicality. The most important thing is that the German resistance demonstrate to the world and to history, that it dared to risk its life in a decisive gamble. Anything else is irrelevant."[47]

In this way, death was an affirmation of life, and failure brought with it a unique nobility. This is what Tresckow said to Fabian von Schlabrendorff on the day after the coup. Tresckow had decided to kill himself in order to protect his family and his friends from reprisals. The moment was one of high drama, and Tresckow delivered his lines, imbued with a striking combination of Christian and classical metaphors, well. "With remarkable calm," Schlabrendorff wrote later, Tresckow said:

> Now they will all fall upon us . . . and cover us with abuse. But I am convinced, now as much as ever, that we have done the right thing. I believe Hitler to be the arch-enemy, not only of Germany, but indeed of the entire world. In a few hours' time, I shall stand before God and answer for what I have done and what I have failed to do. I think I can with a clear conscience stand by all I have done in the battle against Hitler. Just as God once promised Abraham that He would spare Sodom if only ten just men could be found . . . I also have reason to hope that, for our sakes, He will not destroy Germany. No one among us can complain about his death, for whoever joined our ranks put on the poisoned shirt of Nessus. A man's character is proven only at the point where he is prepared to give his life for his convictions.[48]"

The night before, in Bendlerstrasse's courtyard, Claus von

Stauffenberg had faced the firing squad. An instant before he was killed, he shouted something which, to some, sounded like "Long live Germany!" Schiller could not have staged a better death.

The conspirators' complex character is not entirely unfamiliar. As Garry Wills has pointed out elsewhere, "dying well" and the "art of resignation" were integral to, for example, George Washington and the American revolutionaries, and elements of this ethic can be found in the Victorian and the Southern "gentleman."[49] This ethic alone is no protection from evil. It is not incompatible with imperialism, male dominance, and racism; it certainly can serve as a mask for evil; it did not protect the conspirators from complicity in the some of the greatest crimes in modern history. But if this ethic can be manipulated to legitimate evil, it can also subvert the evil it ostensibly legitimates.

In the last weeks of his life, Ludwig Beck discovered Robert E. Lee. Beck was a scholar as well as a soldier and his study of military affairs was extensive. Though a francophile, Beck had decided to improve his English. He began reading Douglas Southall Freeman's four-volume biography of the Confederate commander.

Beck found in Lee a congenially paradoxical figure—a soldier who hated war but who was convinced that waging war was at times a necessary evil; a gentle, impeccably courteous gentleman, who was a ferociously aggressive warrior; a man who prized freedom, but who used his great talents not simply to defend "states' rights," but the evil of human slavery as well; a fundamentally good man, who fought for what must be called a bad cause. Lee's character impressed Beck. Freeman recounts that, toward the end of his life, after the war, Lee was riding "Traveller" in northern Virginia, and a young woman ran out to him. The woman lifted her infant son up to Lee and asked for the general's blessing. The old soldier looked at the child, thought a moment, and gravely said: "Teach him that he must deny himself." Ludwig Beck approved.[50]

At its best, the conspirators' character was remarkable though not historically unique. James Green, in his introduction to an anthology of Thomas More's writings, outlines this character well:

This is the kind of man who achieved that wisdom which allows one to take oneself and history both seriously and not seriously at one and the same time. . . . Men like More are a threat and a scandal to the single-mindedly earnest, to the "true believers." . . . To the single-minded absolutist, anyone who attempts to encompass the polarities of existence threatens the neatness of his ideology. The ironic perspective which sees through the essentially fictitious nature of the social structure, the comic vision which sees simultaneously both the absurdity and the usefulness of our social fictions and rituals, must sooner or later clash with those who cannot live so precariously. The man who punctuates artifice with ironic laughter, who insists on saying no as well as yes, must be forced to mount the scaffold on Tower Hill to face the absolutist's ultimate weapon: the headsman's ax.[51]

4

Vettern

Patriotism, ultimately, determined my actions—my love of
Germany, its centuries of history, its spiritual and political
development. And so, I can stand proudly with my ancestors,
with my father and brothers.
— Peter Graf Yorck von Wartenburg, 1944

Dietrich Bonhoeffer, like Claus von Stauffenberg, wore an unusual ring.[1] It was a family ring, bearing the crest of the Bonhoeffer family. The Bonhoeffers were not aristocrats, but they were
an old family; they even had their own coat of arms.

According to family tradition, the first Bonhoeffers came from
Holland. By the early 1500s, they had established themselves in
Schwäbish Halle, in southwest Germany, as goldsmiths, mer-
chants, pastors, and town officials. In the Michaelis Church in
Schwäbish Halle, paintings of several formidable Bonhoeffers
frown down on the congregation.[2]

Dietrich Bonhoeffer's life orbited about his family. His parents,
seven brothers and sisters, his cousins and in-laws were his intimates, rivals, and supporters. His friends quickly found themselves absorbed into his elaborate family network. He never
married (he became engaged in 1942, but his arrest in 1943 destroyed his marriage plans), and his world was essentially familial.

Bonhoeffer's parents considered real education to be an ac-
quired sense of being heir to a historical tradition. Eberhard
Bethge writes that Bonhoeffer "grew up in a family which
thought that education was not so much a matter of school-learn-
ing, but rather growth in the conviction that one was heir and
protector to a great historical and spiritual inheritance."[3] To
think of oneself as fundamentally an heir meant that whatever
one had inherited from others and had not simply earned needed

to be preserved and honored, not just enjoyed and consumed; that what one had inherited had to be passed along undiminished, and ideally augmented, to the next generation; that above all, one was not an island in time, a kind of monad, but rather that one was an actor in a long and important drama in which one was responsible not only to oneself and the present, but even more importantly, to both the past and the future. All this was embedded in an intense and concrete way in the family.

Bonhoeffer's friends were amazed at his devotion to his family. Even when he was far away, his first thoughts were of home. Erwin Sutz, an exchange student with Bonhoeffer in New York in the early 1930s, had never met anyone who spent so much money on letters, telegrams, and trans-Atlantic telephone calls.[4]

Bonhoeffer was not unique. To understand the conspirators' moral universe, one must understand their relationship to their kin, their "vettern."

The first circle of the conspirators' lives was their family, their "vettern." Their character, in fact, is inexplicable unless it is seen in the context of their families—large, semipublic, loosely woven but remarkably durable fabrics of brothers and sisters, mothers and fathers, grandparents, children, in-laws, cousins, and cousins' cousins.

This is something of a surprise because generational conflict and family ruptures seemed endemic to the late nineteenth and early twentieth centuries. In Germany, around the turn of the century, the war between the generations, especially the often fierce conflicts between fathers and sons, sparked the Youth Movement, obsessed artists, and absorbed the popular press. Robert Wohl has shown just how crucial peer identity, not family loyalty, was in shaping the values of the "generation of 1914."[5]

But here the conspirators were unique. Whatever hatreds might have flared in other families, the conspirators remembered their own families fondly. General Ludwig Beck, Army Chief of Staff in the 1930s, was a reticent man, but he could be almost lyrical when remembering his youth.

His father, Beck reminisced nostalgically, owned a small factory in Biebrich, on the Rhine, and was a model of hard work and reliability. Yet the elder Beck, the general remembered, always had time for his sons, and his parents, Beck recalled, preferred to spend their evenings at home with their children. "Everyone who lived then," General Beck wrote later, "in that home, in that beautiful spot along the Rhine, has innumerable beautiful and unforgettable memories." The Beck household was old-fashioned, patriarchal, traditional, and disciplined—among other things, the future Chief of the General Staff learned "to get up early!"—but even this lesson Beck recalled with love.[6] His brother wrote later about Ludwig Beck that "tradition and spartan discipline, in modest circumstances, shaped the contours of his character."[7]

The Bonhoeffers, though higher in the social scale, were much like the Becks. Dietrich Bonhoeffer's family too was hierarchical and paternalistic. No one doubted that father, then mother, were at the top of the family pyramid, and that the "kids," the twins Dietrich and Sabina, were at the bottom. The elder Bonhoeffers set the family's tone, and Sabina recalled that her father, one of Berlin's leading psychiatrists, "was rather distant and reserved . . . he would stress a point by preciseness, not loudness of speech. . . . He spoke little, and we felt his judgment in a look of surprise, a teasing word, and sometimes a slightly ironical style."[8]

The family communicated by means of an elaborate set of subtle cues, "glances of surprise," and "slightly ironic smiles," all embedded in complex rituals. The Bonhoeffer family dinner, Sabina remembered, was "almost a ceremonious affair."[9]

Conversation in the Bonhoeffer family was serious but lively. Children were expected to participate, but what they said had to be thoughtful, which was why, Sabina observed, "we could not abide clichés, gossip, platitudes, or pomposity when we grew up."[10] Emmi Bonhoeffer, Dietrich's sister-in-law, wrote of the Bonhoeffer home: "In theory, one was liberal in tolerating others' styles of living, but in practice, the English that's not done played so great a part that you felt it as soon as you were inside the porch."[11]

The other conspirators came from similar families. In the Moltke family, the same sort of free, yet disciplined, and in fact "English" style prevailed.[12] Carl Goerderler's "old prussian," "Fredrician," "monarchical" family values stayed with him for life.[13] Claus von Stauffenberg's father, palace marshal of the King of Württemberg, was, one of Claus's friends remembered:

> . . . a devout but not a political Catholic; he looked and was a conservative aristocrat; he was an expert on court ceremonial. . . . He would have nothing to do with sentimentality.[14]

The conspirators' sense of family was also powerfully geographic. Ludwig Beck was convinced that there was nowhere in the world quite like his Rhineland. Helmuth James von Moltke's conspiratorial headquarters was his family estate in Silesia, and his last letters, written from prison, are filled with yearning for Kreisau. In one letter, Moltke recalled his life at Kreisau, calling it "that lovely time which seems to me golden in retrospect, an inexhaustible source of memories on which one draws with affectionate delight and of scenes which I will always treasure."[15] Claus von Stauffenberg boasted, with a little exaggeration, that the only Germans not broken by the Nazis were his fellow Swabians.[16] Henning von Tresckow once remarked that if Wartenberg, his family's estate in Pomerania, were ever threatened, he would resign from the army and give his life to defend his home.[17]

The conspirator's sense of family was also historical and custodial. All the conspirators, not just the aristocrats, felt themselves to be part of an elaborate familial mosaic that stretched both backward and forward in time. Generations of Tresckows, Stauffenbergs, Moltkes, Yorcks, Kleists, and others had molded values and standards that the conspirators inherited, felt themselves bound by, and responsible for transmitting to yet another generation. Violating this tradition was quite literally unthinkable.

Public service, often in the military, was a central element of this inheritance. Yet this family tradition of public service did not demand obedience to any particular political regime, for any regime was itself to be judged in relationship to the longer tradition of public service and family loyalty. Indeed, "treason" to a given regime, in the name of the commonwealth and the family, was something to be honored. Once, for example, someone warned Helmuth James von Moltke that he was liable to be hanged as a traitor. "Well," Moltke responded, "if I am hanged, I shan't be the first Moltke to whom that happened and I hope I shan't be the last."[18]

Loyalty to the past implied responsibility for the future, and the future was incarnated in children. This meant not simply transmitting the family name and property; much more important was transmitting to the coming generation a coherent set of values and a world in which such values could thrive. If the conspirators acted in part because of their ancestors, they acted even more because of their children. In 1942, in an essay circulated to his friends, many of whom were in the conspiracy, Dietrich Bonhoeffer argued that "the ultimate question for a responsible man to ask is not how he is to extricate himself heroically from the affair, but how the coming generation is to live."[19] When he tried to explain why he risked his life in a plot against his own government, Claus von Stauffenberg remarked late in the war: "I could never look the wives and children of the fallen in the eye if I did not do something to stop this senseless slaughter."[20]

Some of the conspirators' contemporaries, Simone Weil, for instance, argued that "rootlessness" was a typical disease of the modern world. Such estrangement from the world, she thought, was at least partly responsible for modern pathologies.[21] This may indeed be true for that archetypically "modern man"—Adolf Hitler. The 20 July Conspirators, however, were neither "strangers" nor "uprooted." They were at home in the world.

The conspirators' families were bewildering tribes of parents and grandparents, siblings, cousins, in-laws, and friends who had become honorary family members. Their families provided them with their values and moral bearings; they served as places of refuge, conspiratorial lairs, and spaces where one could freely talk and plan to act. Finding one's way along this family labyrinth is daunting, but it is a vital exercise for anyone interested in the moral universe of the conspirators.

Consider, for example, the Bonhoeffers.

Pastor Dietrich Bonhoeffer, during the war, was an agent of the Abwehr, German military intelligence. The Abwehr was at the heart of the conspiracy against Hitler. Bonhoeffer's involvement in the Abwehr led to his arrest in 1943 and his execution in 1945.

Bonhoeffer was recruited into the Abwehr, where a distant cousin was already a section chief,[22] by Hans von Dohnanyi. Dohnanyi, a thin young lawyer whose wire-rimmed glasses gave him a decidedly professorial look, had grown up with the Bonhoeffers in the same Berlin neighborhood. Hans and Dietrich had attended the same secondary school, the Grünewald Gymnasium, although Dohnanyi was four years ahead of Bonhoeffer.

Bonhoeffer and Dohnanyi were doubly related: Hans had married Dietrich's sister, Christina; Hans's sister, Grete, had married Dietrich's older brother, Karl-Friedrich.[23]

Two other members of the Bonhoeffer family were also involved in the conspiracy: Klaus Bonhoeffer, and Rüdiger von Schleicher, a brother-in-law. Dietrich Bonhoeffer, Klaus Bonhoeffer, Rüdiger von Schleicher, and Hans von Dohnanyi, were murdered by the Nazis in the spring of 1945.

For a short time in the late 1930s, Dietrich Bonhoeffer had run a semilegal seminary in Finkenwalde for the anti-Nazi "Confessing Church." An indefatigable supporter of Bonhoeffer's little seminary was a fierce old aristocrat named Ruth von Kleist-Retzow, and Bonhoeffer spent many pleasant weekends at the von Kleist family estates. It was there that he fell in love with Ruth von Kleist's granddaughter, Maria von Wedemeyer. Dietrich and Maria had just gotten engaged when Dietrich was arrested by the Gestapo.[24]

The Kleists were an enormous clan, whose most famous member was the great nineteenth-century poet, Heinrich von Kleist. In the 1930s, Ewald von Kleist was editor of a leading conservative newspaper, and a vigorous anti-Nazi. His son, Ewald Heinrich von Kleist, a young lieutenant in World War II who volunteered to assassinate Hitler in 1943, was in the Bendlerstrasse on 20 July 1944. Another Kleist, Bernd, was on Henning von Tresckow's staff in Russian, and yet another Kleist, Peter, was a colleague of Adam Trott, Hans-Bernd von Haeften, and Ulrich von Hassell, in the Foreign Office.[25]

One of the Kleists' many cousins was Henning von Tresckow. Tresckow's aide, and the courier between Tresckow and Stauffenberg, was Fabian von Schlabrendorff. Schlabrendorff, a journalist and lawyer, had written for the elder Kleist's newspaper; the Nazis banned the paper in 1934 because of a hostile article by Schlabrendorff. In 1935, Schlabrendorff acted as legal counsel for Hans von Wedemeyer, who had refused to raise a Nazi flag on his property; in fact, much to his surprise, Schlabrendorff won the case.[26] Schlabrendorff's wife was another granddaughter of Ruth von Kleist, the grand old lady who was Dietrich Bonhoeffer's ally.

Dietrich Bonhoeffer's father, Klaus Bonhoeffer, married Paula von Hase in 1898. The Hases were an old aristocratic family, with cousins scattered throughout Prussia. Dietrich's maternal grandmother, for instance, was Countess Clara von Kalckreuth, who married Karl Alfred von Hase in 1879. Karl Alfred von Hase was court chaplain for Emperor Wilhelm II. He resigned his post when the Kaiser, who insisted on preaching at services, vulgarly called factory workers "the canaille," the "dirty mob."[27] Karl Alfred von Hase's father, Karl August von Hase, was a noted scholar who had actually met Goethe.

Bonhoeffer's uncle, on his mother's side, was General Paul von Hase. General von Hase was the Berlin city commandant in 1944.

Because of his uncle's intervention, Bonhoeffer was first held in an army prison, not an SS prison. General Paul von Hase was also a conspirator. The Nazis killed him in 1944.

When Bonhoeffer's maternal grandmother, Clara von Kalckreuth, married into the Hase family, her sister, Anna, married into the even more famous Yorck family. In 1813, it was a Yorck who led the Prussian rebellion against Napoleon, and Yorcks had been one of Prussia's leading families ever since. Anna Yorck died quite young, and her husband, Hans Yorck von Wartenburg, married another Kalckreuth sister, Helene. Dietrich Bonhoeffer's mother was raised, in fact, by her aunt, Helene Yorck, and as a child, Dietrich spent many happy vacations as "Klein-Oels," the Yorck's Silesian estate. At Klein-Oels, Dietrich met another great-nephew of his aunt Helene, Peter Yorck von Wartenburg. Peter Yorck, together with Helmut James von Moltke, Carl Dietrich von Trotha, one of Moltke's cousins,[28] and several others, organized the Kreisau Circle of resisters.

Peter Yorck's wife, Marion, remembered that one of the earliest meetings between Peter and Helmut von Moltke took place, appropriately enough, at a christening in 1938. The baby was the child of Davida ("Davy") Yorck, Peter's sister, who had married Hans Adolf von Moltke, the son of Helmuth's great uncle, Fritz.[29] At the christening, Helmuth and Peter discovered that they were somehow or other cousins. They discovered as well that they shared similar concerns about the fate of their nation, and that each had a network of friends who shared their concerns.

Another of Peter Yorck's sisters, Renate, married into the Gersdorff family, one of whose members, Rudolf-Christian von Gersdorff, was a key conspirator in the Abwehr.

Peter Yorck was in the Bendlerstrasse on the evening of 20 July 1944, and was taken by the Nazis. They killed him later that year.[30]

Peter Yorck was at the Bendlerstrasse in part because his distant cousin, Claus von Stauffenberg, was there. The Stauffenbergs, like the Kleists and the Yorcks, were a large clan, though the Stauffenbergs were South Germans, not Prussians. Alfred von Stauffenberg, Claus's grandfather, was named a Count ("Graf"), by Bavaria's king, Ludwig II, in 1874. Claus's father, Alfred Graf Schenk von Stauffenberg, was palace marshal for Württemberg's last monarch, King Wilhelm II (not to be confused, to be sure, with the Emperor Wilhelm II). Claus's mother, Karoline Uxküll-Gyllenband, was related to the Yorcks, as well as to the early eighteenth-century Prussian hero, Neithardt von Gneisenau.[31]

There were three Stauffenberg brothers, the twins Berthold
and Alexander, and their younger brother, Claus. Berthold and
Claus were especially close. They enjoyed the same music and
the same poetry; they were admired by the exotic poet, Stephan
George. In 1943, when he was assigned to Berlin, Claus moved
in with Berthold. Berthold was as deeply involved in the conspiracy as Claus. So, too, were their uncle, Nicholas Graf von
Uxküll, and their cousins, Hans Christoph von Stauffenberg, a
diplomat who later served in the Abwehr, and Cäsar von Hofacker, who was also related to the Yorcks.

Fraternal ties were common in the conspiracy. Claus's aide in
the summer of 1944 was Werner von Haeften. His brother, Hans-
Bernd, was an official in the Foreign Office, and a key conspirator.
The Haeftens had grown up in the Bonhoeffer's neighborhood in
Berlin, and were close friends of the Bonhoeffer family; their
pastor was Martin Niemoeller, the minister who played such a
key role in the Christian resistance. Their father, General Hans
von Haeften, had been the director of the National Archives, but
had resigned rather than falsify documents to please the Nazis.
Their uncle was General Walter von Brauchitsch, the Army Commander until 1942. Werner von Haeften died at Stauffenberg's
side on the night of 20 July; the Nazis killed Hans-Bernd a few
months later.

There were many other pairs of brothers active in the resistance. Erich and Theo Kordt, for example, were colleagues of
Hans-Bernd von Haeften's in the Foreign Office. They played a
critical role in organizing the abortive coup of 1938–39. General
Kurt von Hammerstein-Equard was the Army Commander in
1933, and was bitingly critical of the Nazis. Hammerstein died
in 1943, but his two sons, Kunhert and Ludwig, were active in
the conspiracy.[32]

The entire 20 July Conspiracy seemed to consist of kin. General Erwin von Witzleben, whom the conspirators named Army
Commander on 20 July, was joined in the conspiracy by Job von
Witzleben. Friedrich Werner von der Schulenburg, former ambassador to Moscow, was one of the conspiracy's most important
foreign policy advisors. His nephew, Fritz-Dietlof von der Schulenburg, was something of a political eccentric. Fascinated by
radical politics, he considered himself a Communist for a time,
then joined the Nazi party. In the early 1930s, the Nazis named
Fritz-Dietlof deputy police commissioner of Berlin; his enthusiasm for the party waned rapidly, though, and he left the party to
become an active conspirator. Already in the conspiracy were

Fritz-Dietlof's school classmates Peter Yorck and Cäsar von Hofacker, and Fritz-Dietlof's cousin, Ulrich Wilhelm Schwerin von
Schwanenfeld. All were executed by the Nazis in 1944.

Conspirators who were not actually related typically had at
least know each other for years. Dietrich Bonhoeffer and Hans-
Bernd von Haeften had grown up together and had been confirmed into the Lutheran Church together. Fritz-Dietlof von der
Schulenburg, Cäsar von Hofacker, and Peter Yorck were classmates. Helmuth James von Moltke and Adam Trott zu Solz met
in England when they were both students. Moltke also knew
Berthold von Stauffenberg and Hans Christoph von Stauffenberg
before the war when he was preparing for a career in the foreign
service. Similarly, Adam Trott, also preparing for a diplomatic
career, was a colleague of Hans-Bernd von Haeften. Marion Winter and Dietrich Bonhoeffer were classmates in Berlin's Grünewald Gymnasium; Marion later married Peter Yorck von
Wartenburg. Another of their classmates was Klaus Curtius,
whose father had been foreign minister during the Weimar Republic. Klaus's sister, Barbara, married Hans-Bernd von Haeften.

Senior army officers had known each other and each other's
families for decades. Institutions like the War College, and units
like the Potsdam Guards, later renamed the 9th Infantry Regiment, wove these personal relations together.

During the First World War, for example, Ludwig Beck served
on the staff of Crown Prince Wilhelm. One of his colleagues was
Friedrich-Bernhard von der Schulenburg, Fritz-Dietlof's father.
Karl-Heinrich von Stülpnagel was also on the staff; thirty years
later he was Beck's colleague in the conspiracy. Still another staff
member was Rüdiger von der Goltz. Beck was godfather to one
of Goltz's sons. After the war, von der Goltz became a prominent
attorney in Berlin. When General Werner von Fritsch was accused of homosexuality by the Nazis in 1938, Beck, then Fritsch's
chief of staff, called on his old friend Goltz to defend Fritsch.
Von der Goltz was also related to the Bonhoeffers, and was a
personal friend of Hans von Dohnanyi.[33]

One of General Fritsch's subordinates in the 1930s had been a
young officer named Hans Oster. Oster profoundly admired
Fritsch and was horrified by the Nazi effort to smear his old
commander. More than anything else, the Fritsch affair convinced Oster that the Nazis had to be destroyed. As he formed a
covert opposition network, Oster called especially on his friends
from the old army days: Friedrich Olbricht, Erwin von Witzleben, and Georg Thomas, all of whom became key conspirators.

Oster's son, Achim, supported his father, and mobilized his own network of friends, one of whom was Peter Yorck.

Yorck, Helmut von Moltke, and the others in the Kreisau Circle never called themselves by that name; the term was invented by the Gestapo. Instead, the Kreisau resisters simply called themselves "the friends."[34] In his diary, Ulrich von Hassell wrote that the conspirators were a "band of brothers." Hassell was comparing the conspirators to Shakespearean heroes. He was also making a remarkably accurate sociological observation.

The sociology of the July 20 Conspirators is often misunderstood. Some think that the conspirators wer all soldiers, but that is false; most of the conspirators were civilians, though the soldiers were the "executors" of the plot. Others think that all the conspirators were aristocrats. "The list of names of the conspirators sounds like a doomsday roll from the *Almanach de Gotha*," writes J. P. Stern, and Sebastian Haffner echoes Stern's remark.[35] "The characteristic sociology of the conspiracy," according to Joachim Fest, "had as a result that [its failure] meant more than the end of a Putsch. It was the end of the Prussian aristocracy, whose members formed the core of the conspiracy. . . . Seldom has a social group made its "exit from history" more impressively."[36]

But the German people, as Claus von Stauffenberg once remarked, "consists of more than officers and kraut-Junkers,"[37] and so did the July 20 Conspiracy.

"Notables" Hans Mommsen calls the conspirators, and that is the best name for them. They were a mixture of aristocrats and upper bourgeoisie who saw themselves not simply as a social elite, though they were that, but as persons with a unique right and duty to shape public affairs. The 20 July Conspirators, whether aristocratic or bouregois, saw themselves, as Mommsen explains, "as a political leading cast, and their claim to represent the whole as legitimate simply by reason of their social position and concomitant political responsibilities."[38]

At their worst, to be sure, these notables were a monocle-wearing, table-pounding, self-perpetuating clique, determined to preserve their privileges even if that meant the ruin of the nation. Parodied in the nineteenth century, pilloried in the twentieth century, this old notable elite remains the usual suspect rounded up when historians attempt to explain Germany's blunders and crimes.

No single attribute guaranteed entry into Germany's old no-

table elite. Family was extremely important, and the old aristocratic clans certainly were part of the elite. But simple
membership in an old family was no guarantee of acceptance.
Indeed, as Theodor Fontane's novels powerfully demonstrate,
aristocrats who did not live up to the cultural code of the elite
might well be shunned. And, on the other hand, members of the
upper bourgeoisie who did accept the code might be accepted.
Indeed, the cultural code of the notables, this web of habits and
rituals, tastes and values, prejudices and core metaphors, this
imaginative world, far more than mere genealogy, is what defined, limited and empowered the notable elite.

This notable aesthetic was densely real and unmistakable, yet
remarkably difficult to define. Nowhere was it codified, rarely
was it explicit. There were, to be sure, obvious external signs.
Religious values were important. Most notables were Christians,
and Jews and other non-Christians could seldom hope for real
acceptance by the notables. But this certainly did not mean that
all Christians were notables. And this religious conformity was
not inflexible. Notables were not notably pious; while Prussian
notables were Protestant and especially Lutheran, southern German notables were Catholics.

Money, of course, was very helpful, but genteel poverty did
not necessarily bar entry into the elite, and wealth, if possessed
especially by Jews, was no help.[39]

Political opinion was very important—everyone in the elite,
naturally, was a conservative, but, if not taken to an embarrassing
extreme, a certain political eccentricity was tolerated. Pursuit of
the appropriate "cursus honoris" was required; after all, it was
by attending the right schools, and serving in the right regiments
and governmental departments, that one made the connections
one needed in life. Proper marriage, that is, marriage with another notable, was, of course, expected.

The aesthetic of the German notables engendered a densely
ritualized, intensely liturgical sort of behavior, a kind of "deep
play."[40] Their most typical behavior was not so much utilitarian
as expressive. Every gesture was a pantomime; every word, an
oration; every costume, a symbol; every action, a rite.

The elite's aesthetic was powered by a peculiar paradox. At
one moment, this aesthetic enforced a fierce repression. The stiff-
ness, formality, and coolness, so common in the conspirators'
character, was a product of a rigorous suppression of the sponta-
neous, instinctual, personal, and what they called the "primi-

tive." Yet even as it restrained the "vulgar," the elite's etiquette encouraged the playful.

"Play" refers to those nonutilitarian, public, uniquely human rituals which, while obviously artificial, are nevertheless intensely serious. It is "disinterested" in that the players at least implicitly agree to abide by the "rules." Play, in this sense, is narcissism's contrary, for it directs energy away from the private self to participation in the "game." Playing, one does not so much express one's self, as "participate in expressive action"; play is rooted in the tradition of the "theatrum mundi," which "equated society with theater, everyday action with acting. This tradition . . . couched social life in aesthetic terms, and treated all men as artists because all men can act."[41] At the same time, play is not simply egalitarian, for only those can play who know the rules.

Johannes Huizinga calls play

> . . . a free activity standing quite consciously outside "ordinary" life as being "not serious," but at the same time absorbing the player intensely and utterly. It is an activity connected with no material interest, and no profit can be gained by it. It proceeds within its own proper boundaries of time and space according to fixed rules and in an orderly manner. It promotes the formation of social groupings which tend to surround themselves with secrecy and to stress their difference from the common world by disguise.[42]

The notables' aesthetic is better depicted than described, and Jean Renoir paints a particularly compelling portrait of the repressively playful and playfully repressive notable in his 1937 film *Grand Illusion*. One might reasonably object that Renoir portrays exaggerated types, almost caricatures, not real persons; that his old regime characters are hardly "typical" of the much more "modern" July 20 Conspirators. Such cautions are well taken. Nevertheless, Renoir's film characters do incarnate at least the ideal aesthetic that informed the moral universe of the July 20 Conspirators.

The film's action takes place during the First World War. A French officer, Boeldieu, and several of his men, are in a German prisoner-of-war camp administered by the formidable Rauffenstein. Rauffenstein and Boeldieu are aristocrats of the old school. With their monocles and white gloves, they are arrogant, rigid, and icy cold. Boeldieu, for example, agrees to help his

comrades escape. His comrade, Marechal, clearly a member of
the lower classes, tries to thank him.

> *Marechal:* Listen, whatever happens, I'd like you to know all the
> same. . . .
> *Boeldieu:* (cutting him short) But I'm not doing . . . I'm not doing
> anything for you personally. That excuses us from the danger of
> getting emotional. . . .
> *Marechal:* There are certain times in life, all the same. . . .
> *Boeldieu:* (quite abruptly) Let's avoid them, if you please.

Yet, despite, or perhaps because of their reserve, there is something appealing about Boeldieu and Rauffenstein. Both are culti-
vated, well-educated, and multilingual. Above all, though, they
are playful, with the intense seriousness of children.

Rauffenstein, a fighter pilot, had ordered a wreath to be
dropped over the aerodrome of a fallen enemy, to commemorate
the enemy's courage. After being badly wounded, he is, much to
his distaste, made commandant of the prison camp that eventually holds Boeldieu and his men. Rauffenstein is elaborately polite to Boeldieu and his comrades when they arrive at
Rauffenstein's prison castle. Rauffenstein had earlier met Boeldieu when Boeldieu had been captured, and he greets Boeldieu:
"Delighted to see you again, Boeldieu. . . . Gentlemen, your courage and patriotism earn my respect."

Boeldieu and Rauffenstein wage war within elaborate rules.
When a German sergeant roughly searches Boeldieu, for instance,
Boeldieu stenuously objects. The sergeant bruskly replies,
"That's war," to which Boeldieu retorts: "I could not agree with
you more, but there are polite ways of doing it."

Boeldieu creates a diversion so that his men can escape. Rauffenstein shoots him. But even this terrible event is played within
an elaborate etiquette. Rauffenstein spots Boeldieu high on a
courtyard wall, and shouts:

> Boeldieu, Listen! . . . you understand that if you do not obey at once
> and come down, I shall have to shoot. . . . I dread to do that. I beg
> you . . . man to man, come back.

To which Boeldieu replies: "Damn nice of you, Rauffenstein, but
it's impossible."

Their final scene in the film, with its stiff formality, is almost
as amusing as it is touching. Boeldieu is in bed, dying of Rauffenstein's bullet. Rauffenstein is at his bedside.

Rauffenstein: Forgive me.

Boeldieu: I would have done the same thing . . . duty is duty.

Rauffenstein: Are you in pain?

Boeldieu: I would not have believed that a bullet in the stomach could hurt so much.

Rauffenstein: I was aiming at your leg. . . .

Boeldieu: More than fifty yards away, very bad light . . . and then I was running. . . .

Rauffenstein: Please, no excuses. I was very clumsy. . . .

Boeldieu (speaking with great difficulty): Of us two, it isn't I who should complain the most. I'll be finished soon, but you . . . you haven't finished yet. . . .

Rauffenstein: Not finished dragging out a useless existence.

Boeldieu: For a man of the people, it's terrible to die in the war. For you and me, it was a good solution.

Rauffenstein: I have missed it.

This melancholy note pervades the relationship between Rauffenstein and Boeldieu. In the film, Rauffenstein, badly wounded, is held together by braces and bandages. He and his class are dying. Earlier in the film, Rauffenstein had contemptuously commented on the patriotic enthusiasms roused by the war: "Yes . . . modern warfare, the nation in arms . . . the charming legacy of the French Revolution."

Boeldieu: I am afraid we can do nothing to turn back the clock.

Rauffenstein: I do not know who is going to win this war, but I know one thing: the end of it, whatever it may be, will be the end of the Rauffensteins and the Boeldieus.[43]

The aesthetic of the German notables did not prevent the "Rauffensteins" and "Boeldieus" from endorsing fascism. In 1933, the German notable elite, closing its eyes and holding its nose, embraced Adolf Hitler.

Bella Fromm, Berlin's society reporter, chronicled this sordid affair in her diary. She wrote, for example:

January 29, 1932. People from the uppercrust are turning to Hitler. They close their ears to his constant blasts against aristocrats and the privileged and "high society."

August 31, 1932. Nationalists and monarchists . . . first they deserted their emperor. Now they desert the republic and turn to these gangsters. They think they can seize power, using the Brown mob as a tool.

December 16, 1932. It was rather disconcerting to discover [at a formal ball] how many new sympathizers for National Socialism are to be found in the ranks of the old-time nobility.

In March 1932, Fromm had discussed the Nazi danger with Baron von der Heydt, an official of the Thyssen Bank, and a leading notable. Later she wrote:

I took the precaution of placing quite a few of my valuable paintings with foreign museums as a loan," he added thoughtfully. This is typical. They think of National Socialism in terms of the danger to a few canvasses, their own wealth, themselves. They'll regret it one fine day.[44]

The marriage, however, was not made in heaven. Hitler was, to be sure, an anti-Communist, and he promised to preserve all the good old values of German society. But he and his followers were not exactly the sorts of people one was in the habit of meeting socially. Commenting on the relationship between General Werner von Fritsch and Hitler, Harold Deutsch remarks: "Austrian sans-culotte and artistic dilletante confronted ultra-Prussian professional and neither liked what he saw."[45] This relationship was representative of the unhappy marriage between National Socialists and the notables. But the notables, in general, did not protest too much. Most were like Arthur Koestler's "Herr von Z" in *Darkness at Noon*, who remarks: "I . . . agree with the programme of our manikin with the black mustache—if he only wouldn't shriek so."[46]

Hitler and his supporters never lost their contempt for upper-crust "reactionaries." Joseph Goebbels, for instance, noted in his diary on 20 December 1939:

Gauleiter [Gustav] Simon reports. . . . He tells me about his difficulties with the Wehrmacht. The army is still heavily infiltrated by ultra-reactionary . . . forces. . . . [Martin] Bormann inveighes against the Wehrmacht, which is causing the Party a lot of trouble. But we shall have to wait until the war is over before we can settle this problem.[47]

Alfred Jodl, who served during the war as Hitler's chief operations officer, condemned the arrogance of his brother officers. Complaining about the officers' "cold" attitude toward Hitler in the summer of 1938, Jodl wrote: "The root of disloyalty among the generals is their snobbery. They simply cannot believe or obey or recognize the genius of the Führer, because they still see

him as the corporal of the World War."[48] Years later, Otto Ernst
Remer still insisted that the 20 July Conspirators were little more
than snobs: "They were all members of a class that just couldn't
get over the fact that Hitler didn't have a little 'von' in his name,
and therefore wasn't 'standesgemäss' (a 'proper' person).[49]

This contempt was reciprocal. In officers' clubs, in Berlin's
"better" salons, disdain for Hitler was common. The Nazis never
really fractured the notables' class solidarity—as Missie Vassiltchikov wrote in her diary, one rarely saw real Nazis at the better
parties[50]—and at least until 1944 it was rare for one notable to
be betrayed to the Nazis by another notable.

Notables may have ridiculed Hitler, but they also feared him.
Ulrich von Hassell's diary, for example, is laced with worry about
the Nazis's attacks on the old elite:

September 17, 1938. Hitler's speeches are all demagogic and spiced
with sharp attacks on the upper class. . . . The mounting hatred
against the upper class has been inflamed by the warnings of the
generals . . . against . . . war. . . .

September 29, 1938. [Johannes] von Popitz was extremely bitter . . .
he was of the opinion that the Nazis would proceed with increasing
fury against the "upper stratum" as Hitler calls it. . . .

October 19, 1939. There is every evidence that the hatred of the
Party for the nobility and the so-called intelligentsia is growing ever
stronger. While the youth of the nobility is killed in droves, their
class is jeered at. . . . No wonder that more and more people are
firmly convinced, like [Carl] Goerdeler, that Hitler wants to exterminate the nobility and the educated classes.[51]

Understanding the conspirators' "vettern," their complex networks of kin, the social world in which they lived, is central to
any understanding of the conspirators' moral imagination. First,
their kin provided the conspirators with a strong sense of class
interest, privilege, and responsibility. Class interest should not
be confused with moral judgment; indeed, the two are often contradictory. Notable hostility to the Nazis was often rooted in
selfishness, group egoism, and snobbery. Nor should one assume
that there was any genuine consensus among the notables regarding their class interest—the great majority of notables decided
that it was in their best interest to support, not oppose, the Nazi
regime. But the hostility many notables felt toward the Nazis is

important, because it provided a milieu in which active anti-Nazis could work.

Second, and more important, the conspirators' kin networks provided the conspirators with an effective set of cues by which they could judge behavior. These cues were aesthetic, not moral, but they were enormously powerful in at least raising questions in the conspirators' minds about the Nazi regime.

Sometimes these cues were seemingly trivial. The conspirators and their friends were disturbed by the efforts of Nazi sympathizers in the army to replace the traditional use of the third person when addressing superiors (one should say: "the general wants. . . ?") with the familiar (the Nazis preferred the more egalitarian "you want?").[52] It bothered others that the Nazis preferred to use "woman" ("frau") instead of "lady" ("dame").[53] That Nazi officials wore their baggy brown uniforms, instead of tuxedos, to formal occasions, annoyed still others.[54]

Such issues are undeniably trivial, but others were more serious. Nazi vulgarity repelled even those conspirators who agreed with one or another point in Nazi propaganda. Shortly after the Nazi seizure of power, for example, Claus von Stauffenberg and several fellow officers were directed to attend, in uniform, a speech by Nuremberg's Nazi party leader, Julius Streicher. The plan was to demonstrate the unity between the party and the army. Even Nazis found Streicher's obsession with pornographic anti-Semitism a bit much. After World War II, the judges at the Nuremberg War Crimes Trials decided to hang Streicher as much on aesthetic as on legal grounds.

After listening to perhaps half the speech, Stauffenberg ostentatiously rose and stalked out of the hall. He could hardly be described as an anti-Nazi at this point. The National Socialist stress on patriotism, German pride, and a strong defense, all appealed to young Stauffenberg. But Streicher's rhetorical violence, his crude sexual jokes, his utter lack of restraint were powerful cues to Stauffenberg that something was amiss with the movement.[55] And a sense of propriety, of the rightness of things, of what might be called a kind of moral aesthetics, is at the root of Ludwig Beck's outraged exclamation, made in the middle of the war: "What has this swine Hitler done to our beautiful country!"[56]

More was involved here than mere snobbery. The conspirators were convinced of the truth of the aphorism that "le mauvais goût mène au crime," that "bad taste leads to crime," or more abstractly, that civility and morality were somehow clearly related, and that civility includes self-control, courtesy toward others, and good form. This is what Dietrich Bonhoeffer was trying to get at in the section of his Christmas 1942 circular letter that he called "the sense of quality." He wrote:

> Unless we have the courage to fight for a revival of wholesome reserve between man and man, we shall perish in an anarchy of human values. The impudent contempt for such reserve is the mark of the rabble . . . when the feeling for human quality and the power to exercise reserve cease to exist, chaos is at the door. . . . Quality is the greatest enemy of any kind of mass-levelling. Socially, it means . . . a break with the cult of the "star". . . . Culturally it means a return . . . from sensationalism to reflection, from virtuosity to art . . . from extravagance to moderation.[57]

Finally, the conspirators' kin provided them with the indispensible "space" for reflection, communication, and conspiracy. A kind of "atomization" of society was central to the Nazi tyranny.[58] The Nazis seized the mass media and all but abolished public communication; they absorbed or destroyed most nonparty organizations, and paralyzed social communication; Nazi spies and informers, and more importantly, the fear of spies and informers, made even private communication dangerous. Into this vacuum, the Nazis poured a torrent of lies, confusions, accusations, and fantasies. Language itself became twisted and bizarre, as some words, like "folk" and "community" were laden with fascist connotations, and other words, like "liberal" or "international" were demonized. By perverting and manipulating and ultimately destroying communication, the Nazis not only inhibited coherent action, they also poisoned thought. But within the cocoon of their cousins, the conspirators had a space where communication was at least possible, where words and ideas could be used freely, and where action became possible.

The conspirators' kinship network was the incubator of their moral imagination. This hardly means that this network was a bastion of morality. It does mean, however, that a moral imagination could grow within it. And in the circumstances of Nazi Germany, that was something special indeed. Fabian von Schlabrendorff remarked, "For me, and others like me, there was no struggle or hesitation involved in the decision to reject Hitler and his followers from the very start. They went against everything my own upbringing represented, and the traditions, principles and history of families such as mine."[59]

5

Ehre

Honor is unconditional.

—Ludwig Beck

On that humid Thurday evening, 20 July 1944, General Joachim von Kortzfleisch rushed to Berlin's Bendlerstrasse, the headquarters of the coup d'état. Kortzfleisch was the commander of the military district around Berlin, and he had just learned of *Operation Valkyrie*. Hitler murdered! Erwin von Witzleben, retired under a cloud years before, was to be the new military commander-in-chief! SS and Gestapo leaders were to be disarmed and arrested! General Kortzfleisch was an officer of small imagination, but even he knew that something very dangerous was afoot. He told his deputy to do nothing, absolutely nothing, until the situation became clear. Meantime, Kortzfleisch would go personally to Bendlerstrasse to find out what in the world was happening.

The coup was not a complete surprise to Kortzfleisch. Like all senior officers, Kortzfleisch was fully aware of the chronic unrest among the generals. In 1938, at a dinner party, for example, Army Commander Werner von Fritsch's aide exclaimed: "There will simply have to be some shooting between the contending groups. Unless we shoot, we will never get rid of the SS and this whole gang!"[1]

Such sentiments, if not necessarily such heat, were common within the military. Claus Stauffenberg's commander in Africa, General Friedrich von Broich, recalled after the war: "What everyone said to [Stauffenberg] was that everyone agreed: things couldn't go the way they were, that something would have to happen. But no one exactly volunteered to take the lead."[2]

And only a year before the coup, Kortzfleisch's own chief of staff had argued at an officers' dinner:

It simply won't do to look at the situation through rose-colored glasses. The war is lost. But that doesn't even matter any more. The thing we have to do is hang these brown-uniformed criminals from the lampposts. That's the only way we can cleanse the honor of German soldiers and the German nation from the dirt of these people.[3]

Kortzfleisch did not endorse these comments, but neither did Kortzfleisch betray the speaker to the Gestapo.

If Kortzfleisch was not exactly surprised by *Valkyrie*, he was nevertheless very frightened. At the Bendlerstrasse, Kortzfleisch confronted Ludwig Beck, who urged him to support the coup. According to Hans Bernd Gisevius, who was there at the time:

General Kortzfleisch refused to join us. He based his decision on his oath, he said. Beck was furious and he told me that he had said: "Your oath! Hitler has broken his oath to the constitution, his duty to the nation, a hundred times! How can you talk about your obligation to this man who has done nothing but violate his obligations!"

But none of Beck's arguments impressed Kortzfleisch.[4]

The debate was emblematic. The vast majority of German officers supported Hitler until the very end. They claimed that their "honor" bound them to do so. Yet a handful of officers tried to kill Hitler, and they too appealed to "honor." Appeals to honor can, of course, be the last refuge of scoundrels, but to German soldiers, the thing they called "honor" was the compass that guided their behavior, the template through which they viewed the world. Understanding the moral imagination of the conservative resistance requires an exploration of honor. Character and kin provided a foundation for resistance; for the soldiers especially, the "executors" of the coup, honor provided the crucial impetus for resistance. But honor is a hard idea to follow; as the conspirators themselves discovered, it leads down twisting paths to unexpected destinations.

In October 1935, General Ludwig Beck delivered the keynote address at ceremonies celebrating the 125th anniversary of the founding of the German Army's War College. Everyone in Berlin's elite was there. General Walther von Brauchitsch introduced Chancellor Adolf Hitler as the "revolutionary" who had restored confidence and patriotism to Germany. After Hitler's remarks, General Beck made his speech.

Beck called his talk, "Genius Means Work"; the title came from an aphorism attributed to Field Marshal Helmuth von Moltke,

Bismarck's great captain. Beck's theme was that military success comes not from mystic inspiration but from the systematic, rational, disciplined, and dispassionate analysis that the War College demanded of its students. "Systematic thought," Beck told his audience,

> must be learned and practiced. This is what the War College must teach its students. Nothing would be more dangerous than to surrender to spontaneous impulses that have not been thought through. . . . We need officers who have the self-discipline to follow thoughts logically to conclusions, whose character and nerves are strong enough to follow the dictates of reason. . . . Sudden inspiration may, of course, be valuable . . . but it is far less important than the clear, mature judgment of the realities of a situation.[5]

The speech occurred at the highpoint of Ludwig Beck's military career. Beck was fifty-five years old in 1935, and thirty-seven of those years, his entire adult life, he had devoted to the army.

Beck had joined the old Imperial army in 1898, as an enthusiastic eighteen-year old fresh out of secondary school, eager to join Germany's most prestigious profession. Soldiers in Imperial Germany saw themselves as answering a "calling," not simply pursuing an "occupation." Theirs was a "politics of the nation," not just a "politics of interest," at least in their eyes. The officer corps was bound together by a network of legends and traditions that enveloped the merely individual life of the officer.[6] Well into the Second World War, the officer's "calling" retained its appeal; even many seminarians at Dietrich Bonhoeffer's Finkenwalde seminary looked forward to serving as an officer. "Being an officer," Eberhard Bethge wrote later, "still enjoyed an undiminished respect."[7]

Beck spent twelve years as an artillery officer, then, in 1911, he was appointed to the General Staff, and attended the War College. During the Great War, he served for a time on the staff of the Imperial Crown Prince. He returned to the artillery after the war, slowly worked his way up the command hierarchy, and in the fall of 1933, Chancellor Hitler appointed him Chief of the "Troop Office," the disguised General Staff (disguised because the Allies had demanded the abolition of the General Staff after World War I). In July 1935, the "Troop Office" was officially redesignated the "General Staff." And only weeks before his speech, Beck was promoted to full general.

Technically, the office of Chief of the General Staff was not especially powerful. The Chief of the General Staff was the senior advisor to the Army Commander, and the Army Commander, in turn, was subordinate to the Defense Minister, who was responsible for all the Armed Forces, the Army, Navy, and Air Force.

But the Armed Forces in general saw themselves as a kind of school of the nation, the army was historically the premier service, the army's General Staff Corps was the army's elite, and traditionally the Chief of the General Staff was the most prestigious soldier in the army. The Chief of the General Staff was the heir, the symbolic link, to Bismarck and Moltke the Elder, to the grand traditions of Clausewitz, Gneisenau, Scharnhorst, the Prussian reformers, and to Frederick the Great. The Chief of the General Staff was the incarnation of that "community of memory" which bound the officer corps together and guaranteed its legitimacy and privilege in German society. Beck wrote of the office of Chief of the General Staff:

> He is responsible for the theoretical and practical education of General Staff officers; he is equally responsible for the formation of their character and personality. What he preaches he must practice. Any separation between words and deeds would be fatal and would have a devastating effect on the General Staff. Should he ever be in a situation which would cause such a separation between word and deed, he must, after mature reflection, and even if objectively his analysis is false, resign as Chief of Staff. There must be no doubt whatsoever about his integrity.[8]

In the 1930s, Ludwig Beck was personally as well as professionally the most respected man in the German army. He was a small, thin, ascetic man, laconic and Spartan. An American officer who attended the German War College as an exchange student, Albert Wedemeyer, later remarked: "I knew General Beck personally, and I considered him one of the finest men I have ever met."[9] Helmuth Groscurth, who knew Beck in the 1930s, later remembered his "striking personality," and his "remarkable ability to inspire trust."[10] One of Beck's old instructors, General Thaer, remarked years later:

> Beck was an exceptionally gifted soldier. From my first meeting with him, he reminded me of the great [Field Marshal Helmuth von] Moltke. I was the first commander who qualified him for the General Staff, and even then, his similarity to Moltke was striking. That was in the summer of 1911. I was a major then.[11]

After the war, Erich von Manstein, made a similar comment:

"If anyone I ever met reminded me of Field Marshal von Moltke, it was Beck."[12] The Polish military attaché, after meeting Beck in the 1930s, exclaimed, "Mais, c'est Moltke lui-même!"[13] Toward the end of Beck's life, others remarked that he reminded them of "Old Fritz," Frederick the Great.[14] Fabian von Schlabrendorff described Beck this way:

> Beck didn't look like a soldier or General Staff officer at first. He seemed more like a sage. Every word, every gesture, showed how mature he was, how carefully he expressed what he thought was right. His dignity was such that to do or say anything vulgar in his presence was out of the question.[15]

Beck's speech to the War College in 1935 was meant both to reaffirm the officer corps' loyalty to its traditions and to display allegiance to the new regime. It seemed to do both at the time. In retrospect, it did neither.

Beck's speech was, to be sure, peppered with praise for Adolf Hitler, and there is no reason to doubt Beck's confidence in the new chancellor. Even after the bloody Nazi party purge of 1934, and the passage of the anti-Semitic Nuremberg Laws in 1935, Beck remained convinced, or convinced himself to be convinced, that Hitler was basically a conservative patriot like Beck himself. Yet Beck, by 1935, was increasingly skeptical about the regime, and a more precise, if also veiled, critique of the ideological foundations of the führer-state would be hard to imagine. Hitler's claim to legitimacy was, after all, his magical inspiration, and in his attack on inspiration, Beck precisely pitted the traditions of the army against the new "charisma."

Undoubtedly, Beck assumed that the army was loyal to its traditions and to him, as well as loyal to the new regime. He was partly wrong on the second count and completely wrong on the first. In fact, by the 1930s, a "paradigmatic shift" had been completed in the army's sense of honor which would rupture both the army's tie to Adolf Hitler as well as the army's ties to its own past.

The old honor, which Ludwig Beck incarnated, was a prickly sort of thing, contradictory and paradoxical, arrogant and humble, much given to display even as it condemned self-promotion.

Asceticism was the heart of the old honor, part of what Roland Barthes refers to, in an entirely different context, as "the old theosophical pact, which has always compensated power by an ascetic life."[16] Great power, especially access to violence, is seen as legitimate if it is accompanied by restraint. Thus repression, sublimation, and a cult of self-control were integral to the old honor. In the old army, for example, there were rigorous regulations governing what later generations would consider off-duty conduct. Whom an officer could associate with, the person he could marry, the opinions he could hold, the clubs he could attend, the civilian costume he could wear, and especially his posture, his manner, his tone of voice, were all meticulously regulated, not so much by decree as by the officer corps' powerful corporate culture. General Hans Oster, for example, the man who orchestrated the resistance from within the Abwehr, told his Gestapo interrogators:

> In those days, it was a kind of childlike enthusiasm which made us officers of the king. That the monarchy could ever collapse, for us, that was simply unimaginable. We knew nothing about politics. We wore the king's uniform, and for us, that was enough. In the officers' club, it just wasn't done to read ["liberal" newspapers] like the *Berliner Tageblatt* or the *Frankfurter Zeitung*.[17]

These rules reflected not so much the operational needs of the army, as the caste taboos of the German notables, which could be pitiless. Theodor Fontane, the great chronicler of the nineteenth-century Prussian elite, was fascinated by the elite's tribal proscriptions. In his novel *Effie Briest*, for example, Effie, an innocent young girl, is married off to a much older man. She is unhappy, she feels distant from her husband, and becomes entangled in an affair. Her husband, after a duel with Effie's lover, abandons her, and her parents, who clearly love her, nevertheless disown her. Her violation of her class's demand for feminine discipline and subordination ruins her.[18]

Sexual restraint, so important for women, was equally important, if much more rarely enforced, among men. Hans Oster, for example, had had an illicit liaison with a lady when he was a young cavalry officer. To avoid scandal, Oster had been permitted to resign his commission. Although later readmitted to the officer corps as a "reserve officer," he only returned to the "regular" list during World War II.[19]

The more senior the officer, the greater the need for personal asceticism. In the fall of 1937, for example, Ludwig Beck learned that the defense minister, General Werner von Blomberg, intended to marry a woman of easy virtue. Beck was appalled, and fully endorsed Hitler's sacking of Blomberg. Hitler, to be sure, had none of Beck's old-fashioned scruples. He had shown little interest in Blomberg's personal life. Indeed, Hitler had happily attended Blomberg's wedding. Only when Hitler was looking for a good excuse to purge Blomberg, in order to install more pliable people in the military, did Hitler feign outrage at Blomberg's personal life.[20]

Blomberg's ouster was part of Hitler's dramatic purge of the military high command in early 1938. Fearful that the army would not support him fully in the coming war, Hitler was determined to have his own people in the top commands. At the same time that he removed Blomberg, Hitler also went after General Werner von Fritsch, the army commander and Beck's immediate superior.

Himmler and the Gestapo fabricated evidence alleging that Fritsch was a homosexual. Hitler pretended to be shocked, and removed Fritsch from the army command. Ludwig Beck, who knew full well that Fritsch was being smeared, was horrified. Fritsch was, after all, as ascetic as Beck; a charge of secret and uncontrolled homosexuality struck at the heart of the ethic to which Beck and Fritsch ascribed. That the Nazis would spread such a story for their own political gain stunned Beck. In many ways, the Fritsch affair marks the beginning of Beck's break with Hitler.

Beck's own self-discipline was legendary. Beck married in 1916; his wife died of tuberculosis in 1917, leaving Beck with an infant daughter. Beck never remarried. His life was dedicated to the army and to his daughter. He rose early, worked long hours, and his few luxuries were horseback riding and evenings at home. He was precisely the kind of "military monk" that the old Moltke had so praised.

The asceticism was functional, of course—soldiers needed to inure themselves to the privations they would face in combat. But this ascecticism was as much expressive as it was utilitarian, and what it expressed was an allegiance to an elaborate and antique allegory.

The old honor's implicit assumption was that all dimensions of reality were bound together in a stable and fixed order. Each class, each institution, had its distinct role to play in that order. The honorable person was one who, like Chaucer's knight in the *Canterbury Tales*, fulfilled the obligations of his or her estate.

Links were hierarchical in the allegory of the old honor. The individual was subordinate to the family, the family to church

and state, and the church and state to God's law. In the good
society, all the links in this great chain resonated harmoniously;
personal behavior reinforced the family; the family echoed the
values of church and state; church and state reflected the eternal
order of things. The past was the guide to the future, for the
allegorical chain, organic and continuous, stretched not only
across the present, but through time.

There was no neat division between "public" and "private" in
the old honor, since the "private" was both subordinate to and
symbolic of the "public." Conformity to external standards was
the mark of inner goodness. Since honor was external and historical, reputation was vital. A single blemish on one's honor
was all but irreparable. A dishonorable act might be forgiven,
but reputation would be lost forever. Even the suggestion that
one was dishonorable could provoke a furious response.

The old honor often engendered a mindless conformity, but
paradoxically, it could breed a prickly independence as well.
The old honor's corporatist mentality assumed, to be sure, that
all classes were related, but it simultaneously insisted on the
uniqueness, autonomy, and superiority of the leading estate of
"notables."

And just as the notables' honor distinguished them within society, so the officer corps' honor distinguished it within the state.
The corps, in the old days, had not only its own code of behavior,
but its own legal system, its own networks of friends and allies,
and often, its own agenda as well. It was, in its opinion at least,
a co-determiner of policy, not simply a passive tool of policy.
This created, of course, one of the central problems in German
politics, German "militarism," the problem of the military state-
within-the-state, the military that was largely independent of the
political institutions, public opinion, and courts, the military
that actively, and often recklessly, pursued its own agenda.[21]

Passivity, in the army's opinion, was a soldier's greatest sin.
The Germany army's doctrine "auftragstaktik," or "mission-ori-
ented tactics," insisted that maximum authority be located as far
down the chain of command as possible, so that junior officers
could exercise as much initiative as possible. As General Hans
von Seeckt explained in the 1920s, "auftragstaktik" meant "exactly the opposite of giving orders which try to control the details of an operation. Instead, it means giving orders which
identify the mission, provide the means to accomplish mission,
and authorize complete freedom in the conduct of the operation."[22] During World War II, it was a truism among Germany's

opponents that German troops could be counted on to be remarkably aggressive, inventive, and dangerous, especially at the small-unit level, even when in full retreat.[23]

Disobedience, in the name of honor, though hardly routine, was fully endorsed by the culture of the officer corps. It was precisely this which made the army so difficult and dangerous during the Weimar Republic. The army's commander in those days, General Hans von Seeckt, insisted that he and his officers served "the nation," and not any specific government or form of government. In making this claim, Seeckt was not simply being antidemocratic, though he certainly was that. He was recalling the old tradition of independence of the officer corps, and the "notable" class from which it sprang. The army must never be "partisan," Seeckt wrote. "'Hands off the army!' is my call to all parties. The army serves the state, and only the state, because it is the state."[24] Seeckt undoubtedly endorsed the remark attributed to Napoleon that "Prussia was hatched from a cannonball."

The army's saints were Frederick the Great's officers, all of whom were noted for their ferocious independence. During the Seven Years War, in the mid-eighteenth century, for example, Frederick ordered the pillaging of royal palaces in Saxony. Every officer to whom Frederick gave the order refused to obey. General F. C. von Saldern declared to the king: "Your Majesty may send me to attack the enemy batteries, and I will readily obey. But to act contrary to my honor, oath, and duty, is something which my will and conscience do not permit me to do." Lieutenant Colonel Joachim von der Marvitz was cashiered from the army when he refused to carry out Frederick's command. Von der Marwitz would not obey what he considered a dishonorable order and retired to his estates. On his tombstone, Marwitz ordered inscribed: "He chose Disgrace, when Obedience was incompatible with Honor."[25] Cavalry General Hans Joachim von Ziethen once remarked: "My body belongs to the king, my soul belongs to God, my honor belongs to myself alone."[26]

Honor was taken very personally, but shame, more than guilt, was the sanction of the old honor. Given its public, conformist, and corporatist assumptions, an individual's disgrace could bring the entire caste into disrepute, just as the caste's wrongs could embarrass each member.

Fortunately, however, for those who felt bound by the old honor, the possibility that their caste, or the state that their caste considered its possession, could do anything shameful, seemed remote.

The old honor was never openly repudiated. Indeed, soldiers like Beck, Stauffenberg, Tresckow, and others were promoted precisely because they incarnated the values of the old honor. Even rather mundane officers like Werner von Blomberg, who was never part of the anti-Hitler conspiracy, could be almost eloquent when talking about the old honor. The British military analyst B. H. Liddell Hart met Blomberg at a disarmament conference in 1932. Later, Liddell Hart wrote:

> Blomberg was a natural enthusiast, and looked on the profession of arms in the spirit of the knight-errant. He showed an eager interest in new military ideas, especially those that promised new artistry in tactics as a game of skill, but was still enthusiastic about the possibilities of resuscitating the code of chivalry. He became almost lyrical in discoursing upon the appeal of "gentlemanliness" in war. . . . In a better environment he might have proved a greater figure.[27]

General Hans von Seeckt, who struggled to recreate the German army in the 1920s, and in doing so profoundly weakened the Weimar Republic, not only insisted on increasing the role of the aristocracy in the officer corps, but also tried to restore the political and moral autonomy of the corps (even as he flirted with plots to overthrow the republic). Seeckt considered himself to be a "traditionalist"; he was sure of "certain certainties," and had, for example, little regard for the moral confusion that seemed to him to be typical of the 1920s. Historical relativism, which sometimes seemed to justify monstrosities, was not to his taste. As he acidly remarked in his memoirs, "I find it very inconvenient that I am no longer to regard Nero simply as the imperial monster who used to go to bed by the light of a burning Christian, but rather as a wise but somewhat peculiar modern dictator."[28] No one was more eloquent in praising the old honor than Adolf Hitler. Hitler assiduously promised to restore pride in the officer corps. He reestablished courts of military honor, and insisted on the inherent nobility of the profession of arms. He showered rewards on officers. In 1933, for example, there were only forty-four generals in the entire German army; by 1938, there were 285.[29] After the spectacular success in France in 1940, Hitler promoted twelve officers to field marshal, and eighteen to colonel-general.[30] Little wonder that officers were impressed with the new regime.

It was not in the 1930s that the old honor died, nor did the old honor die a single death. It had been dying since at least the mid-nineteenth century, when critics, both liberal and conservative, had struggled to replace the old honor with a new one, an honor more in tune with modern times.

In the mid-nineteenth century, for example, there had been a bitter debate within the army about officer recruitment and training. Traditionalists insisted that family was the key factor in selecting promising young officers. Socially restricting recruitment to the "right classes" would, of course, guarantee the elite's monopoly of power. Ideologically, the stress on family conformed to the essentially corporatist mentality of the old honor; the social legitimacy of the aristocracy in particular was bound up in the profession of arms. In the profession of arms, traditionalists insisted, the right "character" was the essential ingredient in young officers, and only the right families encouraged the right character. Traditionalists appealed to a royal decree of 1808 which declared: "The chief requirements of a good officer are not knowledge and technical ability alone, but presence of mind, rapid perception, punctuality and accuracy, not to mention proper behavior."[31]

Modernizers retorted that the upper classes in general and the landed aristocracy in particular were simply unable to staff the immense officer corps required in a modern mass army. In any case, modernizers insisted, a modern army needed technicans more than "gentlemen."

Above all, traditionalists argued that the officer corps, as the key "estate," should codetermine public policy, especially foreign policy. Modernizers replied that soldiers ought to be technical experts who were the executors, not the formulators, of policy.

The titanic nineteenth-century battles between Field Marshal Helmuth von Moltke and Chancellor Otto von Bismarck dramatized this intense political conflict. Moltke had little use for politicians. "Our diplomats plunge us forever into misfortune," he once remarked. "Our generals always save us." But when Moltke demanded that the army play an independent role in the shaping of foreign policy, Bismarck was furious. To his wife, Bismarck snorted, "The military gentlemen make my work terrifically difficult for me! They lay their hands on it and ruin it and I have to bear the responsibility!"[32] In the end the civilians won that fight, but by the middle of World War I, the generals, led by Erich Ludendorff, had made a comeback, and the military virtually ran the nation. Then, in 1918, with defeat imminent, they beat a hasty retreat back to their barracks and left Germany's ruins to the civilians.

Often the debate about the army focused on apparently minor issues, but these minor issues had an immense impact on the army's sense of identity and honor. This was especially true of the great duel debate.

The debate about dueling reflects a geologic shift from gestural to utilitarian behavior, from the old honor to the new. The debate was about what officers called "Satisfaktionsfähigkeit": the right to give and demand "satisfaction." German, particularly Prussian, officers felt bound, in the nineteenth century, to a "code duello." Not that they actually dueled all that often, to be sure, but officers were convinced that if their honor and dignity were called into question, they not only had the right, but were compelled by a moral obligation to resolve the matter personally, immediately, and violently.

For modernizers both within and without the military, the duel was symbolic of everything barbaric and anachronistic about the officer corps. The duel was based on the assumption that officers had their own code, distinct from the rest of society, that they had a right to resolve their differences personally, without regard to legal institutions. The duel not only offended legal procedure, however; it was also hopelessly dysfunctional. Officers shooting each other over points of decorum hardly had time to manage an immense and complex modern military bureaucracy.

Modernists insisted that efficiency, not decorum, was the vital standard of "good" behavior. That a thing got done was more important than how it was done. Disputes, modernizers argued, had to be bureaucratized and depersonalized. Personal complaints should be settled not simply by the individuals involved, but by the military administrative apparatus. The argument about the duel had been going on for centuries. But by the late nineteenth century, it was finally clear that "Satisfaktionsfähigkeit" was on the last of its many legs.

Traditionalists took the attack on the duel hard. Old Field Marshal von Manteuffel, an incorrigible reactionary, wrote in 1872: "In the army I was brought up in, it simply was not done to ask a judge to get you satisfaction. You got it for yourself. You drew your pistol, and if the other man refused to fight, you had him soundly thrashed by your fellows."[33]

Dueling was slowly abolished; questions of honor and morality were given over to lawyers, bureaucrats, and courts; and a vital component of the old honor died. The old honor had been something officers "carried about with them, and not something they consigned to the keeping of another."[34] In bureaucratizing questions of honor, the army had shifted moral responsibility up the chain of command, away from individuals. Army chaplains increasingly insisted that for the individual honor was internal and private; a man who did no wrong in his private life was an honorable man. And as for larger questions of morality and honor, they should be decided by superiors, not subordinates. Because moral authority rested with commanders, not their subordinates, morality demanded that subordinates' primary virtue be loyalty. The ideal officer was one whose private life was in order, and whose public life was characterized by obedience and loyalty to superiors.

What was well underway by the late nineteenth century was a profound shift from "extroverted class honor" to "introverted personal honor."[35] The ideal officer became the highly trained technician, the "professional," who was privately decent and professionally reliable. Without doubt, such an officer was infinitely easier to command, and far more efficient, than the obstreperous Frederician officer.

Yet clearly something was missing. In 1860, Prince Frederick Charles of Prussia wrote a long essay "on the origins and development of the spirit of the Prussian officer." He pointed out that in Frederick the Great's day, Prussian officers were famous, or notorious, for their independence. Not infrequently, they would actually refuse to obey commands.

> If an officer wanted to convey to someone that honor forbade him to serve under [a commander], he reversed his spontoon. The junior officer would likewise lay about him with his sabre, on the spot, often on duty too, and even in the face of the enemy, if he thought his superior officer had sullied him.

During the Napoleonic wars, scores of Prussian officers went off to Russia in order to continue the fight against Napoleon, even after the Prussian government had officially given up the struggle. In 1813, when Prussia was still technically an ally of Napoleon, General Yorck, on his own initiative, refused to fight against the Russians, and at Tauroggen, signed a convention in which he declared his, and his army's, temporary neutrality. In his essay, Frederick Charles wrote:

> They set their honor above their duty to obey. A similar convention

may be made one day. The officers are capable of doing it again and the example of Tauroggen would encourage them. Nowhere but among Prussian officers is such a thing to be imagined. . . .

The Prince recounted an anecdote to continue his argument:

One day, when a staff officer was duly carrying out an order he had received, a high-ranking general rebuked him, saying, "Sir, the king made you a staff-officer so that you should learn how not to obey."

As for the present, Frederick Charles was worried. The old honor, he wrote "is being undermined . . . by a certain number of senior officers who think they have been chosen to command a pack of servile knaves, not gentlemen. . . . Boot-licking is not punished but is rewarded by success, telling tales commands a hearing . . . instead of being rejected with indignation.[36]

In 1874, Emperor Wilhelm I issued a long order outlining honor's demands. It said in part:

I . . . look to the whole corps of officers of my army to make honor their finest jewel. . . . To keep its honor pure and spotless must be the most sacred duty of the whole Estate. . . . An officer should endeavor to keep no company but that in which high standards are cherished; and least of all in public places should he forget that he will be looked upon not merely as a man of education, but as one who represents the honor and the higher obligations of his Estate. He should keep aloof from all dealing that may reflect upon the good name of the individual or the fellowship to which he belongs; especially from all excess, from drunkenness and gambling, from contracting any obligation that may lead to even the slightest appearance of dishonest conduct, from speculative dealings on the Stock Exchange, from taking part in any commercial enterprise whose aims are not unimpeachable or whose reputation is not of the highest. Never should he lightly pledge his word of honor.[37]

The emperor's order was a stirring reaffirmation of an old notion of honor, a notion rapidly growing obsolete. By the 1930s, the old honor was a sentimental old hymn that everyone sang on the appropriate occasions, but whose words had become increasingly unintelligible.

At first, the handful of officers imbued with the old honor, and the majority imbued with the new, readily accepted national socialism. Officers were instinctive conservatives, and many conservatives were not sorry to see the end of parliamentary democracy in Germany. For many on the political right, parliament had degenerated into little more than a clearinghouse for lobbyists, political parties were nothing more than selfish interest groups, and conservatives were not sorry to see parliament and the party system go. Nor did they mourn for the Communist party or the other institutions of the political left that Hitler destroyed. Manfred von Brauchitsch, a young officer in the 1930s, wrote later: "We rejected the Weimar Republic, and considered it only a temporary way-station. . . . Anti-communism was for us self-evident, communists were simply scum, communism was simply not something open to discussion."[38] Ludwig Beck wrote in March 1933: "I have hoped for a political change for years, and I am overjoyed that my hopes have not been in vain. This is the first flicker of light since 1918."[39]

Yet it would be a mistake to assume that there were no rubs within the Nazi regime. In fact, a series of actions and disputes gradually became chronic and progressively disaffected a growing circle of soldiers and civilians. The bloody party purge of 1934, the Fritsch and Munich crises of 1938, preparations for the campaign in the West in the winter of 1939–40, and for the invasion of the Soviet Union in 1941, atrocities in the East, the massacres of the Jews all drove officers and civilians into opposition.

The effect was cumulative, gradual, and incremental. Problems typically were isolated from their contexts and explained away as simple "errors." In 1934, Ludwig Beck certainly approved of the violent purge of the Stormtroopers, that "dangerous cancre on Germany's diseased body," as he put it;[40] that many others died as well, including two generals, was a cruel but inevitable concomitant of revolutionary times. Claus Stauffenberg referred to the destruction of the Stormtrooper leadership as the "lancing of a boil."[41]

In the early years of the Nazi regime, anti-Semitism embarrassed people like Ludwig Beck, but it seemed to him that this was simply another unpleasant thing that revolutions brought with them.[42] Petty corruption and bureaucratic blunders could be blamed on the people around Hitler, not on Hitler himself; almost to the day of his execution, Carl Goerdeler, the indefatigable prosyletizer of the conservative opposition, remained convinced that Hitler could eventually be made to understand that his policies meant catastrophe for the nation.[43]

Sooner or later, however, the men who became resisters discovered that the petty corruption, ideological imbecility, systematic lies, and ultimately the atrocities, were not isolated errors, but elements of a sinister pattern. And it was this discovery which drove them, in the end, not to oppose this or that person or policy, but the entire regime as such.

Ludwig Beck's career demonstrates this strange and horrifying experience. It was as if the pleasant and routine lights of daily life slowly darkened, and in the darkness of night things began to stir. Oddities began to appear; the oddities became more and more dangerous; these dangerous oddities grew into crimes; and finally, the crimes became a tide, a flood, an inundation.

As Chief of the General Staff, Ludiwg Beck played a central role in German rearmament. He and his superior, Army Commander Werner von Fritsch, created an instrument of remarkable efficiency. Beck fully endorsed rearmament; as a soldier, he was convinced that it was vital to German national security.

Yet an eerie sensation gradually came to haunt Beck, a sense that he was slowly sinking in a morass he did not quite understand. He was upset by Hitler's sudden demand in 1934 that all soldiers and civil servants take a personal oath to him. Beck took the oath, but muttered as he returned to his office, "One cannot do things in this way," and he never forgave himself for taking the oath.[44]

Beck fiercely fought Hitler's plan to create a kind of super-headquarters to which both the Army Commander and the Chief of the General Staff would be subordinate. In this regard, Beck vehemently echoed the elder Moltke. For Beck, the "instrumentalization" of the army, its translation into an unthinking tool of policy, was an outrage. He later remarked to Fabian von Schlabrendorff that in the summer of 1938, Hitler had angrily said to him: "The Wehrmacht is an instrument of politics. I will give the army its mission when the time comes. The army's job is to do what it is told, and not to debate its orders." To which Beck retorted: "For me as Chief of the General Staff, this is unacceptable. I cannot accept responsibility for orders with whose content I do not approve."[45]

Beck was appalled by the sordid calumny, invented by the Gestapo in 1938, that Army Commander Fritsch was a homosexual with ties to the Berlin "demimonde." Fritsch was eventually cleared of these charges, but Hitler used the scandal to remove Fritsch and put his own man in the Army high command. At one point, Beck urged that Hitler take some public action to restore Fritsch's honor. Hitler responded: "It is I who determine how the honor is to be restored." To which Beck replied, "Honor is unconditional, and will not call a halt even before your person."[46]

The Sudetenland crisis followed immediately on the heels of the Fritsch scandal. The Sudetenland was part of Western Czechoslovakia, but its population was largely German. Hitler was determined to act as the protector of these unhappy Germans, and he was eager to use the army to solve this "Czech problem." Beck's opposition, carefully argued in a series of memoranda, reflected at first tactical and operational concerns. But what is remarkable about the memoranda is the constantly expanding context Beck invoked. Beck's objections were at first tactical; then they were strategic; in the end, they became moral. As he insisted in his most famous memorandum:

> The Führer apparently considers a violent solution to the Sudeten problem, by means of an invasion of Czechoslovakia, inescapable. He is encouraged in this opinion by the irresponsible, radical elements who surround him . . . the fate of the nation is at risk. History will condemn the leaders of the Armed Forces of blood-guilt if they do not act according to their conscience and their technical and strategic knowledge. Soldiers' obedience has its limit, where knowledge, conscience, and sense of responsibility, forbid them to execute an order.[47]

Beck urged Army Commander Walther von Brauchitsch, Fritsch's successor, to call upon all the senior generals to resign their commissions rather than execute the planned invasion of Czechoslovakia.

Brauchitsch refused.

In the summer of 1938, Beck alone resigned. Before he left office, he minuted on a memorandum:

> In order that future historians may know my position, and in order that the reputation of the High Command may remain spotless, I, as Chief of the General Staff, wish to add the following to the record: I have refused to endorse any National Socialist adventures. An ultimate German victory is an impossibility.[48]

What is remarkable about Beck's memoranda is not only their constantly expanding perspective, but their heat and their panic. The moral urgency of the conspirators was not that of academicians, but of drowning men, men suddenly aware that the vortex of crime their own government had begun threatened to suck them down as well. Their violent resistance was "reactive," not "proactive"; it was a desperate effort to swim to shore by men who felt themselves being borne off into the depths of a dark sea.

No one wanted to have to resist. In 1941 or 1942, a cousin of Claus von Stauffenberg tried to recruit Stauffenberg into the conspiracy. Stauffenberg was sympathetic, but insisted that first the war had to be won. During a war, one could not even consider such a conspiracy, especially during a war "against communism." Only after the war, Stauffenberg added, could something be done about the Nazis.[49] Ludwig Beck insisted that his opposition in 1938 had, in a sense, been forced on him. He was not a subversive by nature; indeed, when the idea of a coup d'état was first proposed to him, he angrily responded that "mutiny and revolution are words not found in the lexicon of the German soldier."[50]

But they had no choice. What is striking in the notes the conspirators left behind is the increasingly panicked sense of shame and guilt at the regime's behavior, and the gnawing conviction that the horrors committed by the Nazis would redound on the conspirators' own heads. Each of the conspirators attempted in private and individual ways to ease his guilt: they helped individual Jews; during the war, they treated prisoners decently.[51] As Carl Zuckmayer's fictional General von Harras explained:

We each have our own conscience-Jew, or even several, so we can sleep at night. But we can't be free that way. It's self-deception. Of everything that happens to the thousands of others, whom we don't know and can't help, we're guilty too. Guilty. And damned for all eternity. To permit crimes is worse than to commit them.[52]

Consider, for instance, the letters of Helmuth Stieff, the staff officer who accompanied Stauffenberg on the flight to Rastenburg on 20 July 1944:

November 1939. I am ashamed to be a German! This minority, who through their murder and plundering . . . befoul the German name, they will mean disaster for the entire nation. The things they do . . . must wake an avenging nemesis. . . .

January 1942. We all are so guilty, we're all responsible. In all our pain, I can only see the just recompense for all the sins we Germans have committed.[53]

Or Henning von Tresckow's remark to Rudolf von Gersdorff,

on reading Hitler's murderous orders for the campaign against Russia:

> Gersdorff . . . remember this moment. If we cannot persuade the Field Marshals to do everything to rescind these orders, then Germany will have finally lost her honor. The effects will be felt for centuries, and not only Hitler will bear the guilt. Everyone will be guilty, you and me, your wife and my wife, your children and my children, that woman crossing the street, and those children over there playing ball.[54]

The civilians in the conspiracy echoed exactly the same dread. It is a constant in Ulrich von Hassell's diaries, for instance, and in Helmuth von Moltke's letters. Listen, for example, to one of Moltke's letters home:

> October 21, 1941. The day has been so full of horrible news that I can't write collectedly. . . . What cuts me to the quick . . . is the inadequacy of the soldiers' reaction. . . . How can one bear one's share of guilt? In one part of Serbia two villages have been reduced to ashes, 1,700 men and 240 women of the inhabitants have been executed. . . . In Greece, 240 men were shot in one village. . . . In France, extensive shootings are going on. . . . And all this is child's play compared to what is happening in Poland and Russia. How can I bear this and sit just the same in my warm room and drink tea? Don't I make myself into an accomplice by doing this? What shall I say when someone asks me: "And what did you do during this time?" . . . They have been collecting the Berlin Jews since Saturday. . . . A friend of [Otto] Kiep's saw a Jew collapse in the street; when she wanted to help him, a policeman intervened, prevented her, and kicked the body as it lay on the ground so that it rolled into the gutter. Then he turned to the lady with a last vestige of shame and said, "Those are our orders."[55]

In their despair, both civilians and soldiers turned to the army. Among conservative resisters, there was never any doubt that a military coup was the only way out, and that a military coup had to be led by the generals. Again and again, soldiers and civilians turned to senior commanders and pleaded for support. And again and again, senior commanders hesitated, equivocated, and procrastinated.

In 1933, Herbert von Bismarck appealed to General von Blomberg, then Defense Minister, to oppose Nazi policies. According to Fabian von Schlabrendorff:

When Bismarck explained his ideas to him, Blomberg responded that he was an officer, that his duty was to obey, that his duty was to support the policies of his superiors. Bismarck replied: "I came to speak with the Minister, not the General. According to the constitution, you also bear political responsibility, which has nothing to do with your military rank." At that, Blomberg banged his fist on the desk and said: "I forbid this kind of discussion in my office!"[56]

In 1939, the conspirators approached Walther von Brauchitsch, Fritsch's successor as Army Commander. Bruachitsch responded to their overtures: "I won't do anything; but I won't oppose it, if someone else does it. . . ."[57]

In the middle of the war, the conspirators, searching for someone with direct personal contact with Hitler, contacted General Adolf Heusinger, an officer on Hitler's staff. But Heusinger responded: "My God! This is treason! We're bound by our oath and our military duty!" and refused to cooperate.[58]

Why didn't the generals act? Among front officers during the war, the obvious explanation is not only lack of access to the instruments of power, but simple exhaustion. According to Hans Fritzsche, himself a combat commander:

> . . . these brave front officers were frozen into a hopeless indifference, and into very narrow thinking. To an extent, they could be described, in a military sense, as demoralized. . . . I can understand them well . . . they were psychologically and physically exhausted.[59]

But what of senior commanders, both before and during the war? Physical cowardice? No. If their task had been something as simple and direct as leading a charge, most would have easily done it. Brutality? Did they agree with Hitler's genocidal policies? No, most were personally decent enough men, and there is little evidence that they enjoyed atrocities.

Tactical worries about a coup? In part. Often, the officers agreed that "something had to be done," but they refused to provoke a civil war. After all, World War I, they believed, had been lost because of a "stab in the back" by civilians disrupting the war effort at home, and they refused to be considered their nation's assassin. Repeatedly, the operational contradictions of the plot discouraged potential participants. Hitler had to be removed before he perpetrated some catastrophe, but Hitler was successful and popular and any attempt to topple him would provoke a civil war. Therefore he could not be overthrown until he had provoked the very catastrophe the conspirators hoped to avoid.

Moreover, many generals insisted that they first receive guarantees from the Allies that the Allies would not take advantage of the confusion caused by a coup; the Allies responded that first the coup had to occur, and only then might they consider guarantees. Moreover, organizing a coup is an immensely complex task. Troops had to be mobilized, targets identified, and civilian support generated, and all this had to be done in the strictest secrecy in an army filled with thousands of young officers whose politics were at best unclear, as well as under the very noses of the Gestapo. The penalty for a single misstep was death for the conspirators, their friends, and their families. Officers looking for excuses for inaction had plenty from which to choose. Ulrich von Hassell wrote in his diary on 21 December 1939: "The generals were tired of being continually exposed to influence from all sides, and were deliberately shutting themselves away.... The main argument of the generals against action was that there was not yet enough public sentiment in favor of it, and that they were not sure of the officers from the rank of major on down."[60]

Early on, the generals surrendered to fatalism. Werner von Fritsch, defamed by the Nazis in 1938, at first thought of challenging Heinrich Himmler to a duel. But in the end, Fritsch despaired. He bleakly remarked about Hitler and the army to Hans Oster: "What a wonderful instrument this Wehrmacht has become! But this criminal fool may yet manage to employ it for the destruction of Germany and the world." When the war began, Fritsch told a friend that he would go to the front as a "target"; he was killed in action in 1939, leading his regiment in Poland.[61]

The generals "aren't commanders," Helmuth von Moltke wrote, "but technicians, military technicians, and that is a frightful crime."[62] In an April 1943 diary entry, Ulrich von Hassell tried to capture the mood of the generals, who had failed again and again to respond to the pleas of the conspirators:

April 20, 1943. The longer the war lasts the less I think of the generals. They have undoubted technical ability and physical courage, but little moral courage, absolutely no broad world vision, no inner spiritual independence or that strength of resistance which rests on a genuine cultural basis. For this reason Hitler was able to make them subservient and bind them hand and foot. The majority, moreover, are out to make careers in the lowest sense. Gifts and field marshal's batons are more important to them than the great historical issues and moral values at stake. All those on whom we set our hopes are failing, the more miserably so since they agree with all they have been told and permit themselves to indulge in the most anti-Nazi talk, but are unable to summon up enough courage to act.[63]

Cowardice, brutality, and tactical caution may all have had something to do with the generals' refusal to support the coup, but they are not the main reasons for the lack of resistance. The generals did not resist, ultimately, because of a learned failure of the moral imagination. They had learned that honor meant the triad of technical proficiency, private decency, and public obedience, and they were both unwilling and unable to imagine that anyone could demand more of them than this. The old honor's emphasis on public and not private virtue, on independence and not obedience, on character and not technical skill, was unintelligible to them. B. H. Liddell Hart, who knew many of the generals well, wrote of them: "Few . . . resembled the typical picture of an iron "Prussian" soldier . . . many would have looked in their natural place at any conference of bank managers or civil engineers. They were essentially technicians, intent on their professional job, and with little idea of things outside it."[64]

Again and again they insisted that they were honorable, decent fellows, only doing their duty. Hitler's operations officer, General Alfred Jodl, whom the Allies would hang at Nuremberg as a war criminal, insisted in May 1945:

As a soldier I obeyed and I believed my honor required me to maintain the obedience I had sworn. . . . I have spent these five years working in silence although I often entirely disagreed and thought the orders I got were absurd and impossible. I have known since the spring of 1942 that we could not win the war.[65]

Carl Zuckmayer captures this attitude well when he has his despairing General Harras exclaim:

I've never been a Nazi . . . I'm just a pilot. I've earned my own money . . . I haven't married into society, I've never lived on donations from the Party, I've never stolen anything from a single Jew. I've never built myself any villas. . . . As a general or as a circus clown, I've been just a pilot, nothing else.[66]

In quieter times perhaps these would have better men. They were not made for crisis.

The military conspirators became conspirators because they embodied what the army called its proudest traditions. What the

conspirators discovered was that the old traditions they embodied had been replaced by new ones. They simply could not believe that their fellow officers would so abandon them. There
was still enough solidarity in the officer corps to guarantee that
the generals never denounced their conspiring brothers; there
was not enough solidarity to guarantee that the generals would
unite their fates with those of the conspirators.

The resistance of the generals to the conspiracy drove the conspirators into the resistance. There was rarely a single moment
when a man decided he would resist or not. Instead, there were
a series of moments, a chain of frustrations, which one by one
led the conspirators down a path they did not know. In part, the
conspirators' struggle to recruit the generals was an effort to pass
along to the generals the responsibility for resistance. But when
the generals refused to accept the responsibility, the conspirators
were forced to assume it themselves. In not resisting, the conspirators would have to give up their old honor. But in resisting,
they would have to give up their lives. And that they were alone
in all this outraged them.

"We have no real field marshals any more," Claus von Stauffenberg remarked bitterly to a friend, "they all shake in their shoes
and jump to attention when the Führer gives an order."[67] Once,
fellow officers suggested to Stauffenberg that the best thing to do
would be to wangle a transfer to the front; there, one would have
enough to worry about and would not have to fret about political
responsibilities. In a sense, Stauffenberg had done just that when
he had transferred to a combat unit in Africa. But back in Berlin,
he refused to consider the idea. A friend later wrote of Stauffenberg's reply:

> It was nothing but cowardly evasion [Stauffenberg said] and no better
> than Field Marshals using the excuse: "we're only following orders,"
> and "we're only soldiers." An entirely different outlook was needed.
> A man whom office and honor had raised to a position of leadership
> reached a point where he and his task became one, and other consid-
> erations no longer applied: he was responsible for everything. How
> few there were who in fact behaved like that or at least felt they ought
> to! The majority were just petty bourgeois people with a nice income
> . . . holding the rank of general. They were drawing their pay, doing
> their "duty," "trusting in the Führer," and looking forward to going
> on leave.[68]

Recovering from his African battle wounds in 1943, Stauffenberg remarked, "Since the generals have so far done nothing, the

colonels must now go into action."[69] To his wife he said, "As General Staff officers, we all share the responsibility."[70]

Meanwhile, a thousand miles away, on the Russian Front, Henning von Tresckow struggled to convince senior officers to take action against Hitler. "If we don't do it, no one will," Tresckow insisted to Field Marshal von Manstein. "We are responsible. The responsibility is ours."[71] Manstein said no.

"Is it not monstrous," Tresckow remarked to his colleage, Rudolf von Gersdorff, "that here are two colonels on the General Staff of the German army talking about the best way of killing the Head of State? And yet it is the only way to save the Reich and the German people from the greatest catastrophe in their history."[72]

And one winter, while walking with Schlabrendorff, Tresckow pointed to the frozen carcass of a dog. "It won't be long," Tresckow said, "when we will be like that . . . I only wish I could meet our collected military leadership in a room, and tell them that they had no pity, no shame, no conscience. I can't even express my contempt for them."[73]

And all this is why Joachim von Kortzfleisch and Ludwig Beck, two old soldiers, debated about honor in the middle of a coup d'état. The debate was not only between these two men, but between two concepts of honor, both of which had evolved long before either of these men had been born. The new honor had the last word, at least during the war. Only weeks after the failed coup, Hitler demanded that the army convene a Court of Honor to expel the conspirators, both the living and the dead, from the army. A panel of senior officers duly convened, and duly expelled the conspirators from the profession of arms for violating military honor. One of the prosecution's key advisors and witnesses was General Joachim von Kortzfleisch.[74]

6

Anti-Christ

I have hated you [Hitler] in every hour that has gone by, I hate
you so that I would happily give my life for your death, and
happily go to my own doom if only I could witness yours,
take you with me into the depths. When I let this hate free, I
am almost overcome by it, but I cannot change this and do
not really know how it could be otherwise. Let no one depre-
cate this, nor fool himself about the power of such hatred.
Hate drives to reality. Hate is the father of action. The way
out of our defiled and desecrated house is through the command to hate Satan. Only so will we earn the right to search
in the darkness for the way of love.
—Friedrich Percyval Reck-Malleczewen, August 1939

In the spring of 1939, Friedrich Percyval Reck-Malleczewen decided to visit Berlin. Reck-Malleczewen was fifty-five years old,
the son of an old Prussian aristocratic family. He enjoyed the
leisure to engage in scholarly work, and had attempted to write
philosophy. He called his volume *Das Ende der Termiten*, "The
End of the Termites," but never quite completed it. His most
serious thoughts he confided to his diary, and his memories of
his spring trip to Berlin were ghastly.

Reck-Malleczewin visited a friend, the actor Hans Albers. Albers had starred with Marlene Dietrich in "The Blue Angel," and
was for a generation of German women something of a heart-
throb. He had a magnificent apartment in central Berlin, over-
looking the Tiergarten, "filled," Reck-Malleczewin acidly wrote
in his diary, "with questionable antiques which he unquestion-
ably thinks are genuine."

The city was even more disturbing to Reck-Malleczewin than
Albers's nouveau riche apartment. The city was crawling with
soldiers, called in to celebrate the führer's birthday, and "their
hideous boots were visible in front of all the doors." "Berlin,"
Reck-Malleczewin wrote, "smells of war."

102

He visited a West-End nightclub, crowded with boisterous and obnoxious SS officers, all celebrating the holiday. But what horrified him most was a scene in front of the Reich Chancellery.

On Hitler's birthday, downtown Berlin was packed with marching troops and frantic crowds. The mood of the crowd in which Reck-Malleczewin found himself was part carnival, part revival. And when Hitler himself appeared, the crowd exploded with cheers. "There he stood," Reck-Malleczewin wrote in his diary,

> the most glorious of all, in his usual pose with hands clasped over his belly, looking, with his silver-decorated uniform and cap drawn far down over his forehead, like a streetcar conductor. I examined his face through binoculars. The whole of it was all slack and without structure—slaggy, gelatinous, sick. There was no light in it, none of the shimmer and shining of a man sent by God. Instead, the face bore the stigma of sexual inadequacy, of the rancor of a half-man who had turned his fury at his impotence into brutalizing others.
>
> And through it all this bovine and finally moronic roar of "Heil." . . .
>
> I reflected again on this thick-witted mob and its bovine roar; on this failure of a Moloch to whom this crowd was roaring homage; and on the ocean of disgrace into which we have all sunk.
>
> No, the much-maligned generation of the Wilhelms never quite reached this point of adoration of a Chosen One. In this case, it is really true that yesterday's sins were not as bad as today's. No, these are filth! These ceremonials are not anything to be seen and grasped. Satan has loosed his bonds, a herd of demons is upon us.[1]

Reck-Malleczewin was never an active member of the conspiracy, but his attitude reflects well that of the conspirators. Perhaps the most arresting aspect of the conspirators' moral imagination is their growing certainty that what they confronted in Hitler and National Socialism was not inefficiency and incompetence, not bad politics or fanaticism, but evil, raw, conscious, and vicious. Their understanding of Hitler was prepolitical, almost primitive; they saw themselves not as participants in politics, but tragedy, and not only tragedy, but blood-rituals. For they were not only convinced that Hitler had to be destroyed, they were convinced that he had tainted, infected, and befouled them, and that they, too, must die even as they killed him. Indeed, they believed that only by dying in the killing could they save themselves. They hoped as well that their dying, even if Hitler himself survived, might somehow be redemptive for others. This strange, archaic intuition is at the heart of the moral imagination of the conspiracy against Hitler.

In 1933, the Nazis swept into Berlin with the enthusiasm of locusts headed for the cornfield. The Nazi party was an engine fueled by plunder, and party members energetically enjoyed the spoils they had won. Party hacks became state officials; cashiered officers became intelligence agents; ideological primitives became policymakers.

Holding their noses, closing their eyes, Germany's elite embraced the Nazi thugs and bumpkins. After all, conservative politicians like Alfred Hugenburg and Franz von Papen argued, Hitler was a good anticommunist, and while he controlled the mob, they would control him.

Hitler was an anticommunist all right, but he wasn't easy to control; nor were his people.

The first result of the Nazis' "great barbecue" was a wave of petty, and not so petty, corruption. Hermann Goering, Joseph Goebbels, and other party potentates moved into sumptuous villas in Berlin. Every party bureaucrat had to have his own limousine and chauffeur, and each felt quite free to divert public monies to private purposes—the Nazi party became, in fact, a "public corporation," entitled to taxpayer support. Even the most minor party member considered himself at least a swagger superior to mere civil servants. The Nazis were determined to enjoy what a later generation of politicians would call the "advantages of incumbency," and they fought bitterly among themselves for access to the public trough.

Hans Bernd Gisevius was twenty-nine years old in 1933. A young lawyer, Gisevius was hired in July of that year to work for the Prussian police. He was placed in the "political" section, which would quickly evolve into the Gestapo. Gisevius's superior, and the first head of the Gestapo, was Rudolf Diehls.

That summer of 1933, the atmosphere in Berlin was chaotic. When Gisevius reported in August to Gestapo headquarters on Berlin's Prinz Albrechtstrasse, Stormtrooper "thugs" (as Gisevius later described them), blocked the entrance and refused to let him in. Gisevius soon learned that Gestapo chief Diehls had opposed Gisevius's appointment because Gisevius had been active as a young conservative, and Diehls considered him a "reactionary." He also learned that his immediate superior, Arthur Nebe, was at odds with Diehls. Nebe, Gisevius wrote later, "came to the incredible but inevitable conclusion that Diehls, who was chief of the Gestapo, was in reality a Communist in disguise."[2]

Nebe recruited Gisevius into a plot to get Diehls fired. In September 1933, Diehls was fired after reports of killings and beatings condoned or conducted by the Nazi-infiltrated police shocked old President von Hindenburg. Paul Hinker replaced Diehls. Hinker was an alcoholic, and so incompetent, historian Jacques Delarue not incorrectly describes him as a "congenital idiot," who, in October 1933, was in turn fired, and replaced by Diehls.[3]

Meanwhile, reports of murders kept coming in to the Prussian police, but Gisevius was instructed to hush them up. Documents disappeared, and investigations suddenly were cancelled, while officials in one office busily plotted against colleagues down the hall. Gisevius, appalled by the whole business, got himself transferred to the Interior Ministry.

Things were less violent, but no less chaotic, over there. Nazis were contemptuous of both process ("legalism" they called it), and institutions ("mere bureaucracies," they snorted), and they preferred to make policy by "intuition" and "boldness." The anti-Nazi Ernst Fraenkel, in 1940, rather delicately described Nazi Germany as a "dual state." The "normative" state, governed by law, he wrote, was absorbed by the Nazi "prerogative" state, which repudiated constitutional restraints, judicial review, and even formal rationality.[4] The rule of law, though never officially abolished, was overwhelmed by a kind of guerrilla war politics. In the great scramble for booty, party hacks appointed themselves and their cronies to office without the least regard for qualifications or efficiency.

In 1934, for example, Gisevius's new agency, the Prussian State Interior Ministry, was directed by Wilhelm Frick. Frick was subordinate to Hermann Goering, who was the Prussian State minister-president. In the summer of 1934, however, the Prussian State Interior Ministry merged with the national Interior Ministry, though the two different bureaus did keep their distinct identities. Frick became both the national and the Prussian State interior minister. That, of course, created a rather confusing situation. As the Prussian interior minister, Frick was still subordinate to Goering, but as the national interior minister, Frick was superior to State Minister-President Goering—but only in a way. For Goering, as Air Force Commander, minister of the Four Year Plan, and, for that matter, Chief Forest Ranger, was a cabinet-level official, and therefore equal to Frick. This sort of arrangement did not exactly make for administrative efficiency, and the confusion in Gisevius's agency was typical of the state Hitler built.[5]

"Wherever I knocked," Gisevius wrote, "I found the lower officials in the ministries wringing their hands in despair. But none of the ministers had any serious intention of doing anything. All of them were peering toward the Bendlerstrasse to see whether the army was going to come to their aid."[6]

Things were just as bad at the local level. The party grew like a cancerous topsy; it was everywhere, into everything, and party officials and civil servants constantly squabbled over who had what say where. In 1935, for instance, Hannover's chief executive, a professional civil servant, sent a long report to the national Interior minister, in which he complained bitterly about the behavior of local party officials:

> There are repeated complaints from the public that they have no respect for many of the subordinate leaders of the [Nazi] movement. Arrogance, presumption, particularly on the part of the Hitler Youth, morally objectionable conduct, and alcoholic excesses are the reasons for the attitude, with embezzlement added. . . . Some people in authority mistakenly believe themselves to be outside the normal jurisdiction of the police, and that, since they are representatives of the movement, no action, even should they commit offences or crimes, can be taken against them. . . . Cooperation between the party and state and local government officials is sometimes complicated or even wholly frustrated by unsuitable or incompetent Party officials.[7]

When fantacism combined with venality and incompetence, coherent policymaking was impossible. Hjalmar Schacht, for example, early found himself at odds with party officials. Schacht, a banker of international reputation, was the man credited with conquering the horrific inflation of the early 1920s. He was a man of flexible political scruples, and quite willingly agreed to become a key economic advisor to the Hitler government. Schacht, however, continued to think in orthodox economic terms, and he constantly fretted about trade agreements, the balance of payments, currency stability, and so on. He quickly discovered, however, that Hitler had not the least fear of the hard edges of economic reality and that the men around Hitler were economic illiterates.

Hitler, given his intense suspicion of "foreigners," wanted to hear nothing of international trade. To the contrary, Hitler insisted that Germany had been defeated in the Great War largely because of its vulnerability to external economic pressures (which was true) and that the English blockade would never have worked had Germany been self-sufficient (which was also true but irrelevant, since no modern economy can ever be entirely self-sufficient). Schacht tried to point out that economic autarchy was a chimera in an interdependent world; that if Hitler wanted a modern economy, he had to participate in international commerce; that Germany desperately needed vigorous foreign trade; and that prosperous international trade required an orderly and peaceful diplomatic environment. Hitler was not interested. Schacht resigned from the government and drifted cautiously and tentatively into opposition.[8]

Hitler's hallucinatory strategic plans drove Ludwig Beck into opposition in 1938; Hitler's murderous plans for the Russian campaign, and his repeated interference in the minutiae of military operations, drove Henning von Tresckow and his friends on the Eastern Front into the resistance.

Hitler systematically destroyed the state, and the July 20 Conspirators' first objections were managerial and procedural. Critics are quite correct when they argue that the conservatives' opposition to Hitler was tactical. Critics are wrong, however, to assume that the resistance's opposition was only tactical. Their primary objections were not even political in the narrow sense. The conspirators' politics are important. They spent a great deal of time debating policies and procedures, and historians have been right to investigate the conspirators' politics carefully. But something far more incandescent than policies and procedures drove the resisters to conspiracy and assassination.[9]

The Berlin establishment had shed no tears for Communists, union leaders, and other "leftists" arrested in 1933. They dismissed the 1934 party purge as the necessary and inevitable lancing of the Stormtrooper "boil." Some sighed that attacks on Jews were unfortunate but the understandable consequence of "excessive patriotic zeal."[10] But as the regime stabilized in the mid-1930s, it became apparent to all but the most willfully blind that deceit, betrayal, and violence were not revolutionary ephemera, but the very muscle and bone of the National Socialist regime.

In 1934, for example, General Beck was shocked as much by Nazi involvement in the murky Dollfus affair as by the party purge. Austrian Nazis murdered Austrian Chancellor Dollfus, and though Hitler insisted that neither the German government nor the German Nazi party had anything to do with this crime, serious doubts remained. Beck, as Chief of Staff, was deeply concerned with diplomatic affairs, and he realized that the party purge and the Dollfus affair cast Germany in a very bad light. "The events since June 30," Beck wrote, "have provoked shock and disgust. A leader and a regime so cavalier about law is capable of anything in foreign policy . . . our foreign policy situation is hopeless."[11]

In 1937 and 1938, the Fritsch scandal, and the revelations about Hitler's plan to solve the Czech crisis violently, further alienated Beck. He wrote in May 1938:

> The Führer's plans demonstrate once again the utter inadequacy of the existing military command structure. Constant briefing of the Supreme Commander regarding strategy and above all weapons must be conducted; authority and responsibility must be clearly defined. If an effort is not made to achieve change in the current intolerable situation, and if the current anarchy remains the norm, then one can only have the grimmest perspective on the fate of the armed forces and the fate of Germany in any future war.[12]

The anti-Jewish riots of "Kristallnacht," in November 1938, the assault on Poland, and above all, the attack on Russia, demonstrated both Hitler's preference for violence as well as his disdain for the realities of power. When Henning von Tresckow learned of the plans for the Russian campaign, for instance, he said to an aide: "The German army will fight against Russia like an elephant which attacks an ant-hill. The elephant will kill thousands and thousands, even millions of ants; but it will eventually be defeated by the number of ants and be eaten to the bone."[13]

Sometime in the summer of 1942, Claus von Stauffenberg and his General Staff colleagues recognized that the German army had reached a fatal replacement cross-over point, where casualties began to exceed available reinforcements. They tried to tell the führer, but he was not interested.[14]

Frictions with the regime were more than managerial or political. To the conspirators, the very texture of daily life was frayed and torn; it was as if the nation, and they themselves, steeped in blood, were spinning out of control; it was as if the very air had somehow become viscous, and sulferous; it was as if people they thought they knew had become suddenly alien.

Words lost their meanings in the Nazi world. Joseph Goebbels noted in his diary that "the people think primitively. We speak the language the people understand."[15] Bella Fromm, the Berlin reporter, noted in her diary that the Nazis "used words in a strange, brutal fashion. They used slogans that were made up of German words, slogans that had no place in the mind of anyone who was accustomed to the words of Goethe and Heine. The language sounded German. But in its use by the Nazis, it became practically foreign."[16]

This was not a language Helmuth James von Moltke understood. He wrote in 1941: "Words have lost their unequivocal meaning, symbols no longer evoke a uniform concept, works of art have been robbed of their true significance and,—like all cultural values—have become functional. They serve the state . . . and have become relativized."[17]

People, it seemed, lost their souls. One bleak November day in 1940, Moltke sat in Breslau's train station and watched his fellow citizens hurry by. He wrote to his wife:

> . . . all these passers-by were types, not human beings. They were material to be slaughtered or set to work, machines which had a definite function in a process. I literally didn't see another human being except for my very nice porter. The current into which all these people had been dragged had torn them from their human moorings. In Africa one calls this "detribalization" and associates it with the idea that the natives are thereby rendered incapable both of ruling and being ruled. The same thing is happening to us.[18]

Dietrich Bonhoeffer saw it happening from his prison cell. In late November 1943, Bonhoeffer watched the bombing of Berlin from his window in Tegel prison. Tegel was adjacent to the Borsig firm's rail yards, and waves of British night bombers rained fire down on the target and anything near it.

Bonhoeffer was disturbed more by his fellow prisoners than by the bombing. They scrambled for shelter, howled in terror, and when the attack finally ceased, pantingly recounted their fear to each other. Bonhoeffer was aghast. He wrote to his friend Eberhard Bethge:

> Dear Eberhard,
> . . . we've had the expected large-scale attack on Borsig. It really is a strange feeling to see the "Christmas trees," the flares that the leading aircraft drops, coming down right over our heads. The shouting and screaming of the prisoners . . . was terrible. . . . People around here talk openly about how frightened they were. I don't know what to make of it, for fright surely is something to be ashamed of. I have a

feeling that it shouldn't be talked about except in the confessional, otherwise it might easily involve a certain amount of exhibitionism; and a fortiori, there is no need to play the hero. On the other hand, naive frankness can be quite disarming. But even so, there's a cynical, I might almost say ungodly, frankness, the kind that breaks out in heavy drinking and fornication, and gives the impression of chaos. I wonder whether fright is not one of the "pudenda," which ought to be concealed. I must think about it further.[19]

In December 1943, his reading of Adalbert Stifter, the nineteenth-century novelist of whom he was particularly fond, rekindled Bonhoeffer's interest in the nature of exhibitionism. As he explained in another letter to Bethge:

Dear Eberhard,
I've been thinking again about what I wrote to you about our own fear. I think that here, under the guise of honesty, something is being passed off as "natural" that is at bottom a symptom of sin; it is really quite analogous to talking openly about sexual matters. After all, "truthfulness" does not mean uncovering everything that exists. God himself made clothes for human beings. . . . Exposure is cynical. . . . In my opinion, the greatness of Stifter lies in his refusal to force his way into people's inner life, in his respect for reticence, and in his willingness to observe people more or less cautiously from the outside but not from the inside. . . . I remember once being impressed when Frau von Kleist-Kieckow told me with genuine horror about a film that showed the growth of a plant speeded up; she said that she and her husband could not stand it, as they felt it to be an impermissible prying into the mystery of life. . . . "Speaking the truth" . . . means . . . saying how something really is—that is, showing respect for secrecy, intimacy, and concealment. "Betrayal" . . . is not truth.[20]

Bonhoeffer's comments were not idiosyncratic; he had hit upon the peculiar pan-eroticism that fueled National Socialism, and bound together the Nazi fascination with kitsch and death.

Kitsch is good art gone bad. It treats important human concerns, but in a clichéd and trivial way. Kitsch consists of signs, not symbols; nostalgia, not memory; sentiment, not emotion; piety, not faith. But kitsch is not innocent; it triggers Pavlovian responses, and as a substitute for thought and feeling can be immensely powerful.

In a 1939 article entitled "Avant-Garde and Kitsch," the American art critic Clement Greenburg identified the link between kitsch and totalitarianism. "Kitsch," Greenburg wrote, "is a product of the industrial revolution." "Kitsch," he continued, "using for raw material the debased and academicized simulacra of genuine culture, welcomes and cultivates . . . insensitivity. . . . Kitsch is mechanical and operates by formulas. Kitsch is vicarious experience and faked sensations."[21]

Greenburg was fascinated by the political uses of kitsch. "Where today a political regime establishes an official cultural policy," he wrote,

> it is for the sake of demagogy. If kitsch is the official tendency of culture in Germany, Italy, and Russia, it is not because their representative governments are controlled by philistines, but because kitsch is the culture of the masses in these countries, as it is everywhere else. The encouragement of kitsch is merely another of the inexpensive ways in which totalitarian regimes seek to ingratiate themselves with their subjects . . . these regimes . . . flatter the masses by bringing all culture down to their level.[22]

The Nazis were masters of kitsch. Their posters were peopled with firm but caring fathers, nurturing mothers, healthy and obedient children; their rallies glowed with flags and patriotic fervor. Hitler and Goebbels knew that "mass communication" is not necessarily "truth-telling"; even as they disguised their policies and terrorized their opponents, they knew precisely which buttons to push to provoke a sentimental tear in the eye or a patriotic lump in the throat.

Kitsch and death are intimately related. Kitsch might be thought of as a kind of reaction formation, a disguise, an obsessive, stereotypical, ritualized praise of the "wholesome," provoked by an underlying fascination with its opposite. More accurately though, kitsch might be thought of as cousin to violence. Kitsch is nondialogic, noncommunicative, one-dimensional, manipulative, and thus ultimately inhuman; it literally does violence to the human, it transforms the living into the dead, the dynamic into the static, the multidimensional into the one-dimensional, the dialogic into the manipulative, and calls this violence "beautiful." And it does all this because, above all, kitsch is a form of antiart that demands instant gratification. It is this selfish demand for instant gratification, for instinctual satisfaction, for immediate discharge of emotion, which kitsch shares with violence. Both kitsch and violence are both perversely erotic. Both are passionate and emotional, but in a fundamentally inhuman and destructive way.

It is no surprise, then, that the very Nazis who could swoon over kitsch—recurring images of muscular young men, maternal young women, happy, healthy, and wholesome families—could engage in the most ferocious violence. Nazis exuded an air of violence, not only violence of action, but of gesture and word and imagination. Nazi violence, the obsession with the psychic netherworld, with the macabre and occult, seemed to contradict the "healthy" images embedded in Nazi kitsch. But what bound together Nazi kitsch and death was insatiable eroticism. Nazism represented appetite unloosed; reason, etiquette, custom, tradition, all these fetters Nazis unbound in favor of immediate gratification. Both kitsch, with its instant, unambiguous, Pavlovian satisfaction, and violence, satisfied this hunger for instant gratification. And passion unleashed eroticised even violence and death. Kitsch and death, far from being contraries, were intimates, linked by an inexorable eroticism.[23]

The notion that immediate gratification, unrestrained passion, produced chaos was hardly unique to the conspirators. Karl Barth, whose influence on the conspirators was immense if indirect, argued in his commentary on Paul's epistle to the Romans, that "sin" is essentially a return to chaos, and that in the chaotic, sin-charged world, "everything becomes libido . . . life becomes totally erotic."[24]

This is what the conspirators discovered when they attended Nazi revivals. The eruptions of hysteria and passion that Hitler evoked were, to the conspirators, defiling, foul, and frightful. Peter and Marion Yorck, for example, attended the celebrations on 30 January 1933, which marked Hitler's coming to power. Marion wrote later that the experience was somehow eerie ("unheimlich"), and added:

> Peter and I stood next to marchers carrying torches, in the middle of a hysterical mob. We could feel the mass excitement as the Stormtroopers marched by. The experience so disgusted Peter that he never participated in another rally, even out of curiosity.[25]

According to Hans Bernd Gisevius, "All these excesses are typical of mass orgasms. . . . It was the unleashed masses who howled, plundered, tortured, and killed in those days."[26] The novelist Carl Zuckmayer, a friend of the young tories associated with Moltke,[27] wrote of Vienna on the March night in 1938 when Austria was officially united to Germany:

> That night all hell broke loose. The underworld opened its gates and vomited forth the lowest, filthiest, most horrible demons it contained.

The city was transformed into a nightmare painting by Hieronymous Bosch. . . . What was unleashed upon Vienna was a torrent of envy, jealousy, bitterness, blind, malignant craving for revenge. All better instincts were silenced.

"Fresh blood," Zuckmayer concluded, "smells vulgar."[28]

The July 20 Conspirators debated politics to be sure, but their ideas and language increasingly took on a primitive and terrible prepolitical tone. They were undergoing, though they did not quite know it, what Paul Ricoeur calls "ethical terror." With their intense sense of defilement and inexplicable suffering, their fear of vengeance, not only Hitler's but God's, they entered a universe in which "the evil of suffering is linked . . . with the evil of fault," where "ethics is mingled with the physics of suffering, while suffering is surcharged with ethical meanings." They found themselves in the "reign of terror," the "order of dread," the primordial world at the basis of all ethics,[29] in which evil is palpable, fear constant, and violent purification the only hope— the world described so powerfully by Georges Bernanos:

Who would deny that Evil is organized, that it constitutes a universe that is more real than that which is apparent to our senses, with its sinister landscapes, its pallid sky, its cold sun, its cruel stars. A kingdom that is spiritual and at the same time carnal, of a tremendous density, of an almost infinite heaviness, in comparison with which the kingdoms of earth are like images or symbols. A kingdom that can only really be countered by the mysterious kingdom of God which we talk about, alas, without our being able to understand or even imagine, but the advent of which we await.[30]

A cindered, stagnant air had engulfed the nation, the polluted air of ritual tragedy, and "in such a non-conducting atmosphere all purposes are short, hidden, and mistook, and they soon sink into frightened or oblivious stagnation."[31]

Yet, as Dietrich Bonhoeffer wrote, evil ironically "appears in the form of light, or beneficience, or historical necessity or of social justice";[32] it recites the shibboliths so appealing to decent people—"tradition," "patriotism," "duty," "Fatherland," even as it works its subterranean wickedness. "One is distressed," Bonhoeffer added, "by the failure of 'reasonable' people to perceive either the depths of evil, or the depths of the holy."[33]

"I just spoke with Ernst von Weizsacker in the Foreign Office,"

Ulrich von Hassell noted in his diary on 17 October 1939, and "he . . . considers Hitler possessed."[34]

A metaphor, of course. But a year later, Carl Goerdeler made the same point in one of the innumerable memos that he circulated among the conspirators:

> For the honest man there is no salvation but in the conviction that the wicked is capable of all evil. . . . To have faith in the man, of whom it was said with so much truth that he had hell in his heart and chaos in his head, is more than blindness.[35]

Historians have long and rightly resisted any attempt to "demonize" Hitler. He may have been a tyrant or a psychopath or a capitalist tool, or any number of other things, but to demonize him removes responsibility from the shoulders of everyone else; it obscures Hitler's own human responsiblity; it only encourages a fanatical mentality; it might, oddly enough, make him even more attractive. In any case, to transform a bohemian fanatic into a "metaphysical principle" simply translates the entire Nazi experience from the world of rational discourse into the realm of the occult.[36]

Yet to the conspirators, Hitler was more than simply a tyrant, or psychopath, or tool. The conspirators, no doubt, picked up some of their Manicheanism from Hitler himself, and, as James Wilkenson notes, most European resisters during World War II tended to think in very black-and-white terms.[37] Nevertheless, for the conspirators, there was something uncanny and nocturnal about Hitler and everything he touched. He and his party were an eruption into the middle of the twentieth century of something primitive and bestial; they were agents of the ethical terror that overwhelmed the conspirators.

Hitler, the "star" who fascinated millions, exuded something foul and miasmic to the conspirators. Nikolas von Halem, a close friend of Fabian von Schlabrendorff, described Hitler as the "herald of chaos."[38] Ernst Niekisch, a conservative who flirted with socialist ideas, published a pamphlet in 1932, entitled "Hitler— Germany's Doom."[39] Edgar Jung, a leader of the young conservatives, commented angrily in 1931: "I simply can't imagine that this man with a gangster's face could ever be Germany's dictator."[40] "For this Al Capone to become dictator of Germany," Jung wrote, "would be a disaster."[41] In 1941, Helmuth Stieff wrote from his post at Hitler's headquarters: "Every day that passes here strengthens one's dislike of this proletarian megalomaniac

. . . the whole thing is simply disgusting and disgraceful!"[42] Hitler visited the Russian front in 1943, and Fabian von Schlabrendorff wrote later: "Just to see Hitler eat was a remarkably disgusting sight."[43]

When rumors of massacres in Poland first circulated in Berlin in late 1939 and early 1940, Peter Yorck began to refer to Hitler as the "German Ghengis Khan."[44] In the summer of 1940, Ludwig Beck argued heatedly with a Lutheran pastor who had suggested that, after all, Hitler did have some virtues. "I have seen the man," Beck retorted, "and I can assure you that he is one of the most evil men to walk the face of the earth."[45] Claus von Stauffenberg referred to the atmosphere in the führer's headquarters as "foul and rotten" and described Hitler, Goering, and the other Nazi leaders as "psychopaths."[46] In the summer of 1942, Stauffenberg had exclaimed: "I hate the Führer! I hate the whole rabble around him! . . . is there no officer over there in the Führer's headquarters capable of taking his revolver to the brute?"[47] The Stefan George poem that most impressed Stauffenberg was a strange, prophetic lyric called "Antichrist."

In 1939, just before the war, Fabian von Schlabrendorff had a long talk with his cousin, Henning von Tresckow. Schlabrendorff recalled later that the conversation "ended with the conclusion that we had to do everything to bring an end to Hitler and National Socialism in order to save Germany and Europe from collapsing into barbarism."[48]

It simply wasn't enough, Dietrich Bonhoeffer insisted to friends, to console a person runover; one must put a spoke through the wheel.[49] Jesuit Alfred Delp, a member of the Kreisau Circle, argued in 1943 that "No one will believe our preaching of the "good news" of salvation if we do not do everything possible to save people and our time. We cannot, like the priest and the Levite, pass the wounded man by on our way to heaven, and wait for the good Samaratan to come."[50] To the Dutch military attaché, Hans Oster said at the outbreak of the war, "It is my plan—and my duty—to rid Germany and the world of this plague."[51]

But what exactly were the conspirators to do? "Speak out?" Possible in a gentle democracy; impossible in a terrorist state. Wait for a "popular rebellion" against Hitler? A fantasy—the "people," at least a powerful minority, supported Hitler, and the rest were powerless or apathetic. Attempt to kill Hitler? No one could get near him. Wait for the Army to make a coup? The Army would not make a coup. Old Ewald von Kleist remarked in 1933, that:

> People who don't have the courage to reject a man and his crazy demands, a man whose own party would collapse if it were seriously opposed, people who, out of weakness and myopia actually help him take power—well—such people will never have the ability to fight him successfully. No, he will liquidate all these people eventually, and because of them, he will be able to destroy the nation.[52]

Overwhelmed by evil, the conspirators despaired. Ulrich von Hassell's diary, like Reck-Malleczewin's, was the "diary of a man in despair." Hassell spoke with General Werner von Fritsch in December 1938. Hassell wrote bleakly in his diary:

> The substance of [Fritsch's] views is this: "This man—Hitler—is Germany's destiny for good and for evil. If he now goes into the abyss— which Fritsch believes he will—he will drag us all down with him. There is nothing we can do." I objected to this spirit of resignation, but have to admit that I see little ground for hope.

When Hitler ordered the invasion of Czechoslovakia in March 1939, in violation of the Munich accords, Hassell confided to his diary:

> . . . manifest depravity . . . exceeding all limits including those of decency . . . violation of all decent standards. . . . I cannot believe that this can end in anything but disaster. . . .

On Christmas day, 1939, Hassell recorded news from Poland:

> . . . Nostitz, very depressed, told about absolutely shameless actions in Poland, particularly by the SS. Conditions there as regards sanitation defied description, especially in the Jewish district. . . . The shooting of hundreds of innocent Jews was the order of the day.

In February 1940, after a discussion with Beck, Hassell wrote:

> The pernicious character of the regime, above all in an ethical sense, has become ever clearer to Beck. He spoke of . . . a well-known person . . . who had travelled to Poland, where his worst expectations had been exceeded. He had prepared a report which Beck had read. Among other things, it stated that the SS had left 1500 Jews including women and children, in freight trucks for so long that they all died.

Then the SS had forced 200 peasants to dig mass graves and shot all those who had dug the graves.

And in October 1940:

The hungry workers [in Poland] are gradually getting weaker, the Jews are being systematically exterminated, and a devilish campaign is being launched against the Polish intelligentsia with the express purpose of annhilating it.

In March 1941:

The chaos in Europe is increasing; the devil is at work.[53]

Helmuth von Moltke echoed Hassell's grief and confusion. In 1938, he wrote:

I can't stand the inanity of this existence much longer. . . . I have the feeling that I would far far rather starve in a free land than go on trying to keep up appearances here. For that is what we are all doing. We let ourselves be a facade to cover up the atrocities which go on continually and the only reason for it is that we are left alone for a relatively long time before it's our turn to be got at. I've just no more stomach for it.[54]

Two years later, he had not shaken his despair. Constant reports of atrocities moved him deeply. He wrote in October 1941:

How can one know things like this and yet walk about a free man? What right has one to do so? . . . If only I could be rid of the awful feeling that I have let myself be corrupted. . . . Am I to learn this and still sit at my table in a heated room and drink tea? Don't I thus make myself also guilty? What shall I say, when I am asked "And what did you do during this time?"[55]

In the winter of 1941, in the snows of Russia, Henning von Tresckow remarked to Schlabrendorff:

I wish . . . I could show the German people a film: "Germany At the End of the War." Then maybe they would understand the horrors that await them. Then they might agree with me that the "Supreme Commander" has to go. But we can't show the film. And sure as anything, if we ever get rid of Hitler, the people will invent a "stab-in-the-back" legend. Even if we get the most generous peace terms, they'll still say—"ah, if only you hadn't gotten rid of the Beloved

Leader right before the decisive victory, then we wouldn't have had to worry about peace terms at all."[56]

Outwardly, Dietrich Bonhoeffer maintained his aplomb, but especially after his arrest in 1943, Bonhoeffer nearly gave up all hope. From the very beginning of the Hitler regime, a sense of lonliness had plagued him. He wrote to Karl Barth in 1933: "I have the peculiar sensation of standing in a kind of radical opposition to all my friends. . . . I am increasingly isolated."[57]

His prison poems, such as "Stations on the Road to Freedom," "Jonah," and "The Death of Moses," include long meditations on sin and death. He thought of suicide, he wrote, not "because of guilt, but because essentially I am already dead. Conclusion, end."[58]

The conspirators could, of course, have fled, either abroad, or into the details of daily survival. All had the chance to do so.

Goerdeler, Trott, and Moltke all traveled widely in the years just before the war, and their friends often advised them to join the German exiles abroad. Ludwig Beck resigned as Army Chief of Staff in 1938, but he resigned quietly, and for months he seemed to lose himself in retirement. Claus von Stauffenberg insisted that officers should not seek Front assignments simply to avoid the burdens of political decisions, yet he seemed relieved to be sent off to Africa; he called his new assignment his "flight to the front."[59]

Yet one by one they came back. Carlo Mierendorff, a Social Democratic journalist and member of the Kreisau Circle, returned to Germany in 1933 from Switzerland. "What will the workers think if we leave them there alone?" he asked. "They can't go to the Riviera!"[60] Julius Leber, the conspiracy's link to Social Democratic circles, could have fled the country; at the very least, he could have gone into "inner emigration" and safe obscurity. Instead, he became a conspirator. "I have only one head," he laconically remarked, "and I can think of no better cause for which to risk it."[61] Adam Trott was in China in 1938, but he decided to return to Germany. As he explained to English friends:

There are emigres enough who in certain circumstances could help from outside. But there aren't Germans who are determined to stay in Germany to build a front against the others . . . If Germany is ever to be brought back to the community of nations, then it will only be by Germans who have stayed in the country and suffered there with the others all the humiliations and, finally, the defeat which Hitler will bring to the country.[62]

Bonhoeffer's friends arranged for him to get a grant to study in America in 1939, which would keep him out of harm's way. With a heavy heart, he sailed to New York that summer—and promptly turned about and sailed back to Germany. As he explained in a letter to Reinhold Niebuhr:

> . . . I have made a mistake in coming to America. I must live through this difficult period of our national history with the Christian people of Germany. I will have no right to participate in the reconstruction of Christian life in Germany after the war if I do not share the trials of this time with my people. . . . Christians in Germany will face the terrible alternative of either willing the defeat of their nation in order that Christian civilization may survive, or willing the victory of their nation and therby destroying our civilization. I know which of these alternatives I must choose, but I cannot make that choice in security.[63]

The conspirators went home to fight, but more importantly, they went home to die. They had no illusions. "When this colossus Hitler falls," Adam Trott remarked grimly to Peter Yorck in the summer of 1944, "he will carry us all into the abyss."[64] The conspirators hoped until the end that the coup would work, but they knew full well that it almost certainly wouldn't. In the spring of 1944, Henning von Tresckow said coolly about the planned coup that "in all likelihood it will fail."[65] "The frightful thing" for Tresckow, Schlabrendorff recalled, "was the knowledge that it couldn't work."[66] "It's awful," Berthold von Stauffenberg commented, "to know that it can't work, yet that we must nevertheless act for our country and our children."[67]

Claus von Stauffenberg's uncle warned his niece in the middle of the war:

> . . . I must admit to you that I think it is now too late, and the moment is past; naturally, however, although I think this, I am still heart and soul behind this business, for, even though I believe it has in fact no chance of success, it at least has the advantage that we shall have shown the world that some attempt has been made by Germans to rid themselves of these criminals.[68]

And Ulrich Schwerin von Schwanenfeld's son wrote of his father:

In the last days before July 1944, he fully realized that a violent overthrow of the National Socialist regime could not save Germany from catastrophe. Still, in his opinion, even a failed attempt would show that they had not held back from any sacrifice in the effort to free Germany of the spiritual disease of Nazism.[69]

"There is no hope, there is no deliverance," Ludwig Beck said to Friedrich Meinecke during the war, "we must now drain the bitter cup to the end."[70]

The success of the conspiracy was not the real issue at all. Claus von Stauffenberg argued to his friend Rudolf Fahrner that the success of the plot really was not the important point; the conspiracy, Stauffenberg insisted, was a matter of "inner purification, and honor."[71]

In the summer of 1942, Bonhoeffer remarked that there must be "punishment from God," and that "our action must be such as the world will understand as an act of repentence." He added: "Only in defeat can we atone for the terrible crimes we have committed against Europe and the world."[72] "May our deaths," Carl Goerdeler asked in prison, "act as a guilt offering for the German people."[73] Only weeks before the coup, Ludwig Beck remarked:

> The decisive thing is not what happens to one personally. The decisive thing is not even the effect that all this will have on the German people. What is decisive is that for years, crimes untold, murder upon murder, have been committed in the name of the German people, and that it is a moral duty to act with every means at our disposal to bring an end to these crimes.[74]

Like Arthur Koestler's "Rubashov," Beck, suffering from cancer, had developed a phantom toothache in the last months of his life,[75] which gnawed at him like his sense of guilt. "It is necessary," Beck repeatedly insisted, "for us to purge ourselves."[76] On 20 July before Stauffenberg's bomb exploded, Beck talked with Max Habermann, a labor union official and friend of Carl Goerdeler. Habermann recalled: "Speaking with composure, Beck made his views clear. There was only one essential matter at stake: the criminal system must be attacked from within. Then, even if the attempt failed, it would serve to lose the country's burden of guilt."[77]

They attempted the coup and it failed and most of them died. There was little heroic patina to their deaths, little joy and much sorrow in their actions. They faced grim necessity, knowing that they would be destroyed, but with the hope that their blood might somehow atone for the crimes they had committed, and the crimes committed in their name. In his *Ethics*, Bonhoeffer had written: "Only the crucified man is at peace with God. It is in the figure of the Crucified that man recognizes and discovers himself. To be taken up by God, to be executed on the cross and reconciled, that is the reality of manhood."[78]

Four days after the coup failed, Melanie von Bismarck asked Missie Vassiltchikov to arrange a secret memorial service for the 20 July Conspirators, for the dead and for those in peril. Melanie explained that a service could not be held in one of Berlin's Catholic or Protestant churches, it was too dangerous, but since Missie was a Russian Orthodox Christian, perhaps she could arrange a service at her church. Missie agreed. The two women also decided that for safety's sake, only Missie would attend.

Vassiltchikov made the necessary arrangements with her pastor, Father John Shakovskoy. Later she recorded in her diary:

Monday, July 24, 1944. This afternoon I saw Father John. He thought it would be too dangerous to have a service in the Russian church but he has a small chapel in his flat, and we held it there. I was the only person present, and I cried.[79]

7

Gewissen

Who stands fast? Only the person whose final standard is not reason or principle or conscience or freedom or virtue, but who is ready to sacrifice all this when called to obedient and responsible action in faith and in exclusive allegiance to God, the responsible person, whose entire life is an attempt to answer the question and call of God. But who are these responsible people?

—Dietrich Bonhoeffer

Christmas 1942. The fourth year of the Second World War, the tenth year of Adolf Hitler's Reich.

Christmas 1942 was a joyless Christmas for Germans. In North Africa, by early November, Field Marshal Erwin Rommel and his Afrika Corps were stumbling backward after their bloody defeat at El Alamein. Only days after the end of the battle, American troops landed in Morocco, and the Africa Corps was caught in a Anglo-American vise. On the Eastern Front, a titanic battle was underway around Stalingrad. By the end of November 1942, the German Sixth Army at Stalingrad was trapped and doomed. On the frozen North Atlantic, the tide in the U-boat war had finally turned, and the German submarine wolfpacks, once the hunters, were themselves being hunted down and destroyed.

The last Jews of Berlin were rounded up during the winter of 1942–43. Deportations had begun in October 1941, and by the spring of 1943, Berlin's Jewish community would be destroyed. Rumors swept Berlin about the Jews's destinations, rumors of murder and atrocity, rumors of death factories, rumors of genocide. In October 1942, Helmuth James von Moltke wrote to his wife, Freya, that he had spoken with an SS man about wild stories of huge ovens in Eastern Europe that devoured thousands of human beings. "I hadn't believed it before," Moltke wrote, "but he assured me that it was true. In these huge ovens 6000 human beings can be 'processed' every day."[1]

By the summer of 1942, at least one million five hundred thousand Jews had been murdered in Eastern Europe. By the end of the year, perhaps another one million were slaughtered. In December 1942, the U.S. State Department, together with the other Allied governments, issued a report entitled "The German Extermination of the Jewish Race," which warned that should the exterminations continue, the perpetrators "shall not escape retribution."[2] The exterminations continued another three years.

Allied bombers were systematically destroying Germany by 1942. In August 1942, Missie Vassiltchikov, on her way to a wedding in Bavaria, wrote in her diary:

We passed through the Ruhrgebiet, which is the industrial heartland of Germany, and where many towns are now mile after mile of ruins. In Cologne only the cathedral was still standing. We continued up the Rhine valley past those well-known mediaeval castles, the ruins of which are somehow almost beautiful compared to the ghastly havoc man is causing everywhere nowdays . . . then came Mainz, 80 per cent of which is said to be destroyed.[3]

Friedrich Reck-Malleczewen was in Munich that fall. On 30 October 1942, he wrote in his diary:

I watched the first bombing of Munich from a hotel room . . . a hideous red glare, transforming the autumn night and its full moon. I heard in the distance the muffled booms . . . finally, the whole of the sky to the west was a gigantic sheet of fire. . . . There is some eerie, impending thing in the air, the whole psychical structure of our lives seems to have broken down under the weight of . . . never-ending lies . . . everything is out of joint. . . . And H., with whom I philosophized today about man's inhumanity to man? He has just come back from the Eastern Front, and witnessed the massacre at K., where 30,000 Jews were slaughtered.

This was done in a single day, in the space of an hour, perhaps, and when machine-guns bullets gave out, flame-throwers were used. And spectators hurried to the event from all over the city, off-duty troops, young fellows . . . the night lies black over our heads.[4]

By the fall of 1942, German resistance to Nazism was moribund. There was no organized popular resistance; institutions which could have resisted, such as the labor unions and political parties, were long since dead, their leaders imprisoned, exiled, or murdered. The churches offered no resistance. In 1939 to be sure, the churches had frightened themselves, and the regime, by their vocal opposition to euthanasia. The regime backed away from euthanasia, at least temporarily; the euthanasia killers were sent to new tasks in Eastern Europe, and the churches resumed their silence. The generals, who had seriously plotted a coup in 1938 and 1939, were busy with the war. After the startling victories of 1939–41, officers like Ludwig Beck, who had argued that another war would result in a German catastrophe, were thoroughly discredited. Isolated or in small groups, resisters survived, but by Christmas 1942, they were alone and powerless.

Ulrich von Hassell, one of the leaders of the conspiracy against Hitler, wrote in his diary that fall of 1942:

> There is no hope that any power will appear that can halt this insane machine . . . the moral chaos grows even among the best people. . . . I was told that one should not do anything foolish, that we should just pray. Rely on Jesus.[5]

Nineteen forty-two had been an intense year for Dietrich Bonhoeffer. He was struggling to write his study of Christian ethics, but his writing was constantly interrupted by his work for the resistance.

Bonhoeffer had joined the Abwehr in October 1940. Ostensibly, he was to help the German war effort by using his wide range of church contacts throughout Europe as sources of intelligence. In fact, Bonhoeffer was a clandestine operative for the resistance. He was a courier for Hans Oster and Hans von Dohnanyi, the key conspirators in the Abwehr. In mid-April 1942, Bonhoeffer and Helmut James von Moltke visited Norway and Sweden for the resistance. Their mission was to establish contact with representatives of the Allies, and inform the Allies of the plans of the resistance. Both Bonhoeffer and Moltke were convinced Christians, Abwehr operatives, and resisters, but they differed profoundly on their approaches to resistance. Moltke vigorously opposed plans for a military coup; Germany needed a revolution in the wake of a defeat, not a last minute "putsch," he argued. Bonhoeffer had become convinced that a coup was Germany's, and the world's, best hope. Moltke was already planning the first meeting of resisters at his Kreisau estate, and almost certainly he invited Bonhoeffer to attend.

Bonhoeffer could not attend because he had another mission for the Abwehr. In May 1942, Bonhoeffer was sent to Switzerland to consult his contacts there; in early June, he was back in Scandanavia, and in late June, he was in Italy on a mission with his brother-in-law Dohnanyi.[6]

That Christmas of 1942, Bonhoeffer wrote a short essay as a gift for his friends in the resistance. He called his essay, "After Ten Years." It is a meditation on resistance. It is not an abstract, systematic essay. Instead, Bonhoeffer wrote,

> . . . I should like to try to give some account of what we have experienced and learnt in common during these years—not personal experiences, or anything systematically arranged, or arguments and theories, but conclusions reached more or less in common by a circle of like-minded people, and related to the business of human life . . . the only connection between them being that of concrete experience.[7]

"After Ten Years" is a grim essay. "One may ask," Bonhoeffer writes, "whether there have ever before in human history been people with so little ground under their feet."[8] In recent years, he continues, there has been bravery and self-sacrifice, but "civil courage hardly anywhere, even among ourselves."[9]

> There is hardly one of us who has not known what it is to be betrayed. . . . The air that we breathe is so polluted by mistrust that it almost chokes us.[10]

It is an essay too of confession.

> We have been silent witnesses of evil deeds; we have been drenched by many storms; we have learnt the arts of equivocation and pretence; experience has made us suspicious of others and kept us from being truthful and open; intolerable conflicts have worn us down and even made us cynical. Are we still of any use?[11]

One of Bonhoeffer's central concerns is the question—"Who stands fast?" in the face of evil. One after another, Bonhoeffer recounts those who have failed: "reasonable" people, moral fanatics, people of conscience, persons driven by duty, people dedicated to freedom, persons of private virtue. Each has failed. "Who stands fast?" Bonhoeffer asks. His answer is:

> Only the person whose final standard is not reason or principle or conscience or freedom or virtue, but who is ready to sacrifice all this when called to obedient and responsible action in faith and in

exclusive allegiance to God, the responsible person, whose entire life is an attempt to answer the question and call of God. But who are these responsible people?[12]

These "responsible people" were Bonhoeffer and the July 20 Conspirators. They were the people whose resistance was ultimately grounded in their exclusive allegiance to God. Their resistance was a "rebellion of conscience," an "Aufstand des Gewissens," a rebellion especially of Christian conscience. That was the point Helmuth James von Moltke stressed to his wife. I have been condemned to death, Moltke wrote, "not as a Protestant, not as a landlord, not as a noble, not as a Prussian, not as a German. . . . I have been condemned as a Christian, and for no other reason."[13] The next pages will recollect voices heard in previous pages, and will attempt to trace in the threads of the conspirators' lives the tapestry of their conscience. The voice of Dietrich Bonhoeffer will be especially prominent. Bonhoeffer was not, to be sure, the "typical" conspirator, but his work does reflect a unique and extended reflection on the ethics of conspiracy by a conspirator. And his work finds many echoes, if faint and sometimes unsure, throughout the conspiracy.

To claim that the July 20 Conspiracy was a "rebellion of conscience" does not claim any special piety, virtue, or wisdom for the conspirators. It is, however, to claim that their action was the outcome, first of all, primarily of ideas, not interests.

The distinction between ideas and interests is, if abstract, nevertheless, important. One can argue that human behavior is the outcome of interests. People act the way they do because of their class, because of their desire for power, wealth, status, or simply personal survival. A clear and predictable line can be drawn from the stimulus of interest to the response of behavior. Indeed, human activities triggered by interest might best be described as "behavior" rather than "action," and much human history is the story of "behavior" rather than "action."

"Action" refers to choices and decisions which are the fruit of ideas. Ideas, that complex realm of values, metaphors, prejudices, and convictions, are not synonymous with interests. To defend the reality of ideas and their importance in history is not to argue for occult forces. It is simply to point out that humans can think and speak, that their thoughts and words are related to values, and that thoughts and words and values can produce action.[14] John Maynard Keynes, himself hardly a stranger to the power of interests in human affairs, argued in a famous passage:

> Practical men, who believe themselves to be quite exempt from any intellectual influences, are usually the slaves of some defunct economist. Madmen in authority, who hear voices in the air, are distilling their frenzy from some academic scribbler of a few years back. I am sure that the power of vested interests is vastly exaggerated compared with the gradual encroachment of ideas.[15]

A "hermeneutics of suspicion" has its place. It is, indeed, the typical contemporary hermeneutic. But, as Ernst Bloch has written, the contemporary habit of "demystifying" all too often becomes a form of reductionism, a false form of demystification, which becomes, in fact, a new breed of mystification.

> The fatal category of "nothing-other-than———" belongs in this false kind of demystification . . . and "nothing other than———" will not permit an idea . . . to appear. . . . Certainly the reduction or "tracing back" of every intelligible thing to what is most alien to it, to what at best inspired it or started it off, is a form of vulgar matrialism that is death to the spirit.[16]

The ideas which motivated the 20 July Conspirators were essentially religious ideas, couched in the language of Christendom. These Christian ideas, which might be described as "conscience," motivated their actions. Their rebellion was a rebellion of Christian conscience.

But to defend the priority of ideas is hardly to deny that ideas have a sociological context. The conscience of the conspirators was formed within the nexus of family, profession, and nation.

Perhaps the most important quality of the conspirator's background was its unique balance between "relationality" and "responsibility." Relationality, the sense of living with others in specific contexts and institutions, was a powerful part of the conspirators' conscience. Each had been formed by a "beloved community," especially by their family and their profession. The conspirators felt an intense loyalty to these communities. Indeed, their participation in these communities must be seen as a kind of "vocation," and not "occupation." Being a member of a specific family, being a soldier or diplomat, or lawyer, or pastor, was a thing of great importance.

It was this sense of importance that shaped the intense sense of responsibility, of "living for others," which characterized the conspirators. They were not only responsible in the sense of being dependable and reliable duty-bound men. They felt themselves responsible for the survival and the values of their "beloved communities." This sense of responsibility enabled them to bracket their private needs and fears, to see their private personalities in the context of institutions and communities. Their irony, their ability both to take themselves seriously and not seriously, is itself a product of this interplay of relationality and responsibility.

Behavior can be typical, recurring, predictable, and paradigmatic. Historians interested in such behavior, influenced by the social sciences, search for pattern, the typical, the everyday, the usual. But action is inherently unique; action is always an incident, not a paradigm. Though never "typical," action can be admonitory, even revealing.

The resistance of the July 20 Conspirators was odd. During the Second World War, resistance to Nazism anywhere, and especially in Germany, was unusual. There were differences, to be sure, between Eastern Europe and the Soviet Union, where opposition to Nazi genocide was fairly widespread, and Western Europe, where opposition was much rarer than collaboration. Certainly in Germany, after 1933, opposition to Hitler was rare.

Terror is one explanation for the lack of resistance. *State terrorism works.* When the state uses all of its powers to attack opponents, opposition collapses. Nazi terrorism worked not only because it threatened the lives of opponents, but because it threatened the lives of anyone and everyone associated with the opponent. A resister had to reckon with endangering spouses, children, parents, siblings, and friends. Terrorism worked as well because it was unpredictable and unknowable, yet omnipresent. Everyone, it seemed, was convinced that their phone was tapped, that there were policemen shadowing them or that the midnight knock on the door was coming tonight. The cost of resistance was very high.

Stupidity, and "banality," as Hannah Arendt argued, is equally important in understanding the failure of resistance. Banality, narrow-mindedness, ignorance, and willful stupidity, what Bonhoeffer called "folly," seemed especially dangerous. In "After Ten Years," Bonhoeffer writes:

Folly is a more dangerous enemy to the good than evil. . . . Against folly we have no defense. Neither protests nor force can touch it;

reasoning is no use; facts that contradict personal prejudices can simply be disbelieved . . . people *make* fools of themselves or allow others to make fools of them. . . . One feels in fact, when talking to [the fool] that one is dealing not with a person but with slogans, catchwords, and the like. . . . The person is under a spell, blinded . . . [and] having thus become a passive instrument, the fool will be capable of any evil and at the same time incapable of seeing it is evil.[17]

Even more sinister than folly was enthusiasm. Joachim Fest is right to point out that "those to whom Nazism chiefly appealed were people with a strong but directionless craving for morality."[18] The revivalist quality of Nazism, its remarkable success in achieving a kind of sudden personality change; its conquest of Germany's patriotic symbolism, its ability to pose as the party of family, tradition, law and order, religion, and nation, all made it a powerfully attractive force. Nazis did not simply do wicked things knowing they were wicked things. The greater evil of Nazism was that it translated evil into ostensible good. Peter Haas argues that describing the Holocaust in particular as radical evil, or as the product of "banality," is inadequate. What occurred in Germany, Hass writes, is that Nazism transformed ethics, redefined evil as good, and thus "the perpetrators of the Holocaust (including all its silent witnesses) knew what was going on, found it to be at least ethically tolerable, and consciously acted accordingly."[19]

Perhaps the most remarkable aspect of the Nazi experience was this conquest of ethics by malice. To the conspirators it was extraordinary that malice—greed, envy, resentment, anger, hatred, violence, and murder—is in a palpable sense real. Not only is malice real as a kind of personal fault, but real as a pervasive cultural poison. And, given the right conditions, malice could be justified, legitimized, applauded, and even described as good. In Germany, this poison penetrated everywhere, sickened everyone and everything, transformed persons, twisted organizations, and propelled the policies of the nation. That such a "tyranny of malice" is a theoretical possibility is well-known.[20] That it could actually happen so suddenly and totally was dizzying. "The great masquerade of evil has played havoc with all our ethical concepts," Bonhoeffer wrote to his friends.

For evil to appear disguised as light, charity, historical necessity, or social justice is quite bewildering to anyone brought up on our traditional ethical concepts, while for the Christian who bases his life on the Bible it merely confirms the fundamental wickedness of evil.[21]

The response to all this was a mass withdrawal into "survivorship." Empathy shrivelled; perspectives narrowed; any sense of responsibility and care shrank to the narrowest possible definition; trust and concern was reserved only to intimates; anything outside the most intimate circle was the subject of indifference or suspicion. Again and again, potential resisters encountered this "coyote mentality" among their colleagues and associates. Again and again they collided against a wall of fear and apathy.

"Who stands fast?" Bonhoeffer asked. Only the person whose final standard is exclusive allegiance to God.

The conspirators were all raised as Christians. Few were notably pious. But in the crisis of the 1930s and 1940s, they turned again and again to the one ethical compass in their possession, Christianity. They repeatedly argued, not without ambiguity, that somehow Christianity should inform both resistance to Nazism and the values of a post-Nazi state. But Christianity was important to the conspirators because their existential crisis drove them to theological reflection, and this reflection led them to recover the core themes and metaphors of Christianity. Christianity provided the conspirators with the outline of a cosmic drama in which they, often unwillingly, had become central players, a drama spun out around five core themes: conviction, grace, call, redemption, and hope.

When the conspirators searched for a single concept to embrace their experience of Nazism, they spoke of chaos. In 1936, for example, Helmuth James von Moltke attended a showing of Leni Riefenstal's epic of Hitler's Olympics, *Olympiade*. The film contains little overt Nazi propaganda; it is, however, a hymn in praise of the New Germany, muscular, sensual, and yet oddly detached and cold. Technically, the film is quite impressive. Moltke, though, was disgusted. The endless shots of masses of people horrified him. "And the worst of it is," he wrote, "is that so many people, from whom one might have expected something better, participated in it, and didn't even realize how disgusting and degrading it all is. It was as if I had seen the Anti-Christ personified."[22]

Moltke's reaction, visceral as much as intellectual, echoes the experience of most of the conspirators. Peter and Marion Yorck von Wartenburg witness a Nazi march, Adam Trott attends a Nazi rally, Claus von Stauffenberg listens uneasily to a lecture by Nazi propagandist Julius Streicher, and in each case, the response is revulsion, the eerie sensation that chaos, almost an orgiastic chaos as Fabian von Schlabrendorff wrote, is loose.[23]

Certainly the conspirators' social position may have given rise to their fears of Nazi chaos. As "notables" they certainly looked askance at mobs in the streets. Yet their fear of Nazi chaos was much more than sociological, for Nazism penetrated, polluted, and poisoned what Dietrich Bonhoeffer called the "orders of preservation."

The conspirators were persons with a profound loyalty to social institutions, particularly to family and profession. Their sense of ethical identity was rooted in loyalty to family, loyalty both to their ancestors and their heirs, and to their professions. In both cases, they felt themselves participating in a "vocation," an ethically charged way of life. Theologians had long argued that such social institutions were part of God's plan for human life, part of God's "orders of creation." Bonhoeffer took exception to the term "orders of creation" when pro-Nazi theologians began to use the term to deify race and state. All human institutions, Bonhoeffer argued, are tainted by the fall, all are tempted to sin, none are as God intended them to be. At the same time, however, Bonhoeffer insisted that human institutions, though sinful, are part of God's way of "preserving" human beings in their fallen world. We find God's will through these institutions, in which our lives are intimately entwined with others. The "orders of preservation," or "mandates," as Bonhoeffer later called them, provide the texture of the Christian life, and since we encounter Christ in the encounter with others, the institutions in which we encounter others are of vital ethical importance.[24]

And these institutions, these "orders of preservation," were under assault by the Nazis.

All the conspirators hoped that church and state would resist Nazism. Neither did. Soldiers hoped that the military would resist Nazi penetration. It did not. Before their very eyes, the conspirators saw institutions they deeply loved capitulate before Hitler, and violate their own identities. Their disappointment, grief, and outrage at the failure of especially church and state is a constant theme in their letters and diaries. If this failure was, on the one hand, a salutory lesson in the fraility of all things human, it was also a terrifying moral collapse. For if institutions like family, church, and state genuinely were "orders of preservation," vital to doing God's will, and if they fell into sin, then the key preservations from evil would be gone.

In "After Ten Years," Bonhoeffer desperately warns that human relations are on the verge of disaster. His thoughts are inspired by his conviction that the "orders of preservation" ought to provide patterns of right ethical behavior, and that at the heart of such right behavior was a respect for the other expressed in restraint of the self. But with the collapse of the "orders of preservation," such reserve and restraint is lost. In "After Ten Years," Bonhoeffer writes:

> Unless we have the courage to fight for a revival of a wholesome reserve between person and person, we shall perish in an anarchy of human values. . . . When we forget what is due to ourselves and to others, when the feeling for human quality and the power to exercise reserve cease to exist, chaos is at the door . . . the business of Christianity . . . today will be to defend passionately human dignity and reserve. . . . Socially [this] means . . . a break with the cult of the 'star.' . . . Culturally it means a return from the newspaper and the radio to the book, from feverish activity to unhurried leisure, from dispersion to concentration, from sensationalism to reflection, from virtuosity to art, from snobbery to modesty, from extravagance to moderation.[25]

Early in the war, Moltke repeatedly wrote about the chaos, the disaster, and the catastrophe he was sure was coming. "I'm simply disgusted by the frivolous and incompetent way laws are made today. It's really horrifying. . . . A catastrophe is hurtling toward us. . . . I slept miserably, because at the moment I'm so obsessed with the struggle to avoid the catastrophe awaiting us." By 1940, Moltke was convinced that "evil has triumphed."[26]

The chaos Nazism loosed on the world had an even more frightful side. Just as the "orders of preservation" helped one live morally, their perversion inevitably involved one in their sin. And it was consciousness of sin, of entanglement in evil, of inescapable guilt, which haunted the 20 July Conspirators. "We have been silent witnesses of evil deeds," Bonhoeffer writes, and his sense of complicity and guilt reflects the fears of the conspirators. Responsibility and guilt plagued them: Germany's guilt, and their own.

The "ethical terror" of which Paul Ricoeur writes has its origins in a profound sense of impurity, a conviction of sin and guilt. It was this conviction that made all the difference for the conspirators. It haunted them. They were driven to conspiracy not by class interests or political agendas, but by their own exhausting conviction of sin. They were convinced that Nazism had fractured person, world, and spirit, that they were fragmented, atomized, and disintegrated.

Faced with such a conviction of guilt, one might assume that the ethical response would be to search out timeless moral truths and apply them to the concrete situation. That there are "timeless truths" might seem obvious to any student of ethics. That ethical decision means applying these truths to situations seems to be at the heart of ethical reflection.

But this is precisely what the conspirators did not mean. To be sure, the conspirators did invoke the "higher law." But it would be a serious misreading of the conspirators in general, and a complete misunderstanding of Dietrich Bonhoeffer, to place them in the context of the "higher law" tradition. Few conspirators had the time or the inclination to speculate about the implications of the "higher law." But Dietrich Bonhoeffer did, for him the issue was of immense importance, and for Bonhoeffer, at least, any appeal to a "higher law" is a perversion of Christian ethics.

Even as he disappeared on secret missions for the Abwehr, Bonhoeffer sketched what he hoped would be a book on ethics. At the heart of his book was a vehement repudiation of the "higher law" tradition.

Any discussion of God, truth, and moral value, Bonhoeffer conceded, relies on metaphor, and the spatial metaphor, which places God and Divine Law "higher," and "up there," is not entirely without merit. Perhaps the most ancient way of thinking about God has been spatial, with God thought of as "above" and humanity "below." But for Bonhoeffer, in the crisis of the Second World War, such spatial metaphors had exhausted their meaning.

Bonhoeffer rejected "two-sphere" thinking first because it violated both the entire thrust of the Bible's understanding of God and the distinctively Christian sense of incarnation. The God of the Bible is not an abstract God, not simply a timeless principle or "force" or "entity," but an active, angry, personal, condemning, and redeeming God. To be sure, "eternity" is one dimension of God's reality, but even that is learned only through God's revelation of himself in human history. The Bible is not an almanac of fixed rules and unchanging principles; it is an account of extraordinary actions occurring in time. And at the heart of Christianity is the conviction that God became human in time, in the person of Jesus. To speak of God as if God were a "metaphysical idol," uninvolved in human affairs, might satisfy a Deist, but it could not satisfy, in Bonhoeffer's mind, a Christian. We cannot think of God as "out there" or "up there"; guided by the incarnation, we must think of God as here, now, acting, vital, and present in human history. "I believe that God is no timeless fate, but that he waits for and answers sincere prayers and responsible actions."[27]

Two-sphere thinking is wrong because it is not "concrete." To be "concrete" was enormously important for Bonhoeffer. The church, he insisted, must either be silent or be concrete. He had no desire to turn the church into an arbiter or commentator on mundane politics; he had no desire to turn the preacher into another political agitator. Nevertheless, Bonhoeffer was convinced that the church and the preacher must speak about conviction, conversion, and obedience now, in the present, in the context of the enormous complexities of "concrete" human affairs. The refusal to speak concretely, the flight to "eternal, timeless truths," which too easily turn into toothless platitudes, actually permits the evils that the abstract truths presumably reject.

Two-sphere thought, which concentrates on the application of timeless rules to specific action, is untrue to the ethical experience. Ethics, whatever its cognitive components may be, is something different from a lawyerly debate about rules. Indeed, the very assumption that human beings and human institutions can know the eternal verities is a temptation to arrogance and idolatry, a failure to recognize the fallenness of the world.

The appeal to "timelessness" does injury to the future, and the future is where God's will is expressed. The future was, for Bonhoeffer, a fundamental ethical category. God's will, Bonhoeffer argued, reveals itself in time. God acts in time. This means that the future is the locus of God's will and action. If we are to live in accord with God's will, we must look not only to actions in the immediate present, but to the consequences of those actions for the future. Bonhoeffer is not just narrowly "pragmatic" here, but he shares with pragmatists their conviction that the relative morality of an action only becomes clear in light of its consequences. This means, to be sure, ethical uncertainty in the present, since we cannot know the future. It means as well, though, that ethical reflection must occur in time, and that the future is the focus of ethical reflection.

We must take our share of responsibility for the moulding of history, in every situation and at every moment, whether we are the victors or the vanquished. One who will not allow any occurrence whatever to deprive him of his responsibility for the course of history— because he knows that it has been laid on him by God—will thereafter achieve a more fruitful relation to the events of history than that of barren criticism and equally barren opportunism. . . . The ultimate question . . . is not how one is to extricate oneself from the affair, but how the coming generation is to live.[28]

And later in "After Ten Years," Bonhoeffer writes, "there remains for us only the very narrow way, often extremely difficult to find, of living every day as if it were our last, and yet living in faith and responsibility as though there were to be a great future."[29]

Bonhoeffer was certainly no enemy of law. His own life, and that of his friends in the conspiracy, was marked by an intense sense of order and discipline. But order and discipline come not from legalism, not from "timeless principles" enunciated by an abstract God. Order and discipline are rooted, Bonhoeffer insisted, not in law but in grace.

Grace took the form of an unconditional call that all the conspirators experienced.

This unconditional call was neither mystic nor auditory; none of the conspirators claimed to have seen any visions or heard any voices. There was nothing occult or magical about it. It was nevertheless real, insistent, and powerful. It took the form of a constant tug, a nagging doubt, an insistent conviction that something in their lives was profoundly wrong and that it had to be made right. Indeed, what moved the conspirators was in a sense "pre-ethical." This had little to do with the cool application of timeless principles to specific "cases"; it had much more to do with the experience of guilt and sin and the call to repentant action.

The first striking thing about this unconditional call was its externality, its objectivity.

Crucial to the objectivity of this unconditional demand was the role of Confessing Church, and especially the Barmen Declaration of 1934. In the early years of the Hitler regime, pro-Nazi Christians, the so-called "German Christians," attempted to take over the institutions of the German Protestant churches. Their opponents, eventually called the "Confessing Church," issued a declaration at their conference in Barmen, which explicitly and starkly stated the conflict between Nazism and Christianity. This Barmen Declaration, inspired especially by Karl Barth and Martin Niemoeller, insisted that:

> Jesus Christ, as witnessed to by Sacred Scripture, is the Word of God, whom we hear, whom we trust in life and death, and whom we obey. . . . We reject as false teaching, the claim that the church should recognize as the source of its proclamation events, powers, forms or truths other than the Word of God. . . . We reject as false teaching the claim that the State can, exceeding its proper role, become the single and total source of order for human life, thereby replacing the church.[30]

The language of the Barmen Declaration, with its stark contrast between the claims of Christ and the claims of the state, provided the language with which the conspirators again and again described their motivation. During his treason trial before Judge Roland Freisler, Peter Yorck, for example, tried to explain his actions in the words of Barmen:

> Yorck. Mr. President. I have already explained in my interrogation that, with regard to the development of National Socialism. . . .
> Freisler (interrupting). . . . that you don't agree with it! To be specific, what you said was: with regard to the Jewish Question, you don't agree with the liquidation of the Jews, that you don't accept the National Socialist idea of law. . . .
> Yorck. The most important thing is, what binds all these issues together, is the total demand of the State on the citizen which excludes his religious and moral obligation to God.[31]

These "religious and moral obligations to God" were, to the conspirators, as to the authors of the Barmen Declaration, objective, unconditional, and non-negotiable.

The second striking thing about this call was its intensity. One can refer to it as "conscience," to be sure, but in a sense, the term "conscience" is too private and subjective. While intensely personal and concrete to be sure, this call did not seem to arise merely from the subjectivity of the conspirators. To the contrary, virtually every conspirator attempted to evade, avoid, ignore, and rationalize away this nagging and insistent summons.

Claus von Stauffenberg, for example, found much that was attractive in Nazism. Its appeal to patriotism, to self-sacrifice, to romantic generational rebellion, convinced young Stauffenberg that National Socialism had much to offer. His first sensations that something was wrong—for example, his disgust with Julius Streicher's salacious anti-Semitism—did not make him an anti-Nazi. When encouraged to oppose the regime, he counseled caution and delay. It was important to restore order in Germany; later it was important to win the war; then it was important to muster the support of the general officers. Yet no matter how vigorously Stauffenberg tried to avoid opposition, he could not escape the hounding of this call. Finally, Stauffenberg engaged in the conspiracy, convinced that in some fundamental way he had no other choice.

Ludwig Beck had the same sensation. As Chief of the General Staff in the early Hitler years, Beck did his best to ignore the seamy side of the Nazi regime, the boorishness, the incompetence, the anti-Semitism, even the murders. But Beck could not escape the gnawing conviction that he had to do something, if only to still his own sense of guilt evoked by this sensation of a call. On 20 July 1944, the night of his death, Beck insisted that he and the conspirators had had to act, that they had no other choice, that utilitarian calculation had become invalid.

There were, to be sure, great variations among the conspirators. Some, like Bonhoeffer, were anti-Nazi at least as early as 1933. Others, like Fritz von Schulenburg, were actually pro-Nazi for several years. But in each case, the experience of the confrontation with an unconditional call, in some sense external to them, hounded them into opposition.

This unconditional call was fundamentally a call for integrity. One of the ironies of the Nazi experience was that in the name of integrity, the Nazis shattered integrity. Hitler insistently called for wholeness, for unity, for national rebirth, for "one folk, one nation, one leader." Nazi rituals were paeans to homogeneity and unanimity. Nazis pledged to overcome divisions of class, religion, gender, and ideology by advancing a set of "super-ordinate" values that were prior to and more important than these divisions. Nazis claimed that they would restore family virtues and traditional values and a civic culture of patriotic self-sacrifice.

What Nazism produced was the contrary. What Nazism produced was a profound rupture between the private and the public, between private decency and public brutality, between outward conformity and inward opposition, between word and deed, between truth and lie, between citizen and citizen, between person and conscience. Most Germans learned to live with the resulting "cognitive dissonance" by rigidly compartmentalizing their lives. Privately, within small groups, they could remain reasonable and decent people; publicly, they could not only tolerate but participate in extraordinarily unreasonable indecencies. This is why, for example, the question about "how many Germans knew" about genocide is misphrased. Many Germans had the opportunity to know a great deal. Nazi anti-Semitism was obvious from the beginning. Nazi violence toward political opponents and toward Jews was inescapable. Rumors of the beginnings of the Holocaust were widespread almost as soon as the slaughter began in the summer and fall of 1941. Yet, if many people could know a great deal, few people wanted to know anything, and most found ways to avoid or ignore what they could and did know.

The conspirators attempted to transform, to re-create the fragmentation they experienced in the world around them. They hoped that they could use lies, deception, and concealment to overcome lies, deception, and concealment. They hoped their violent act would bring an end to violence. They hoped that their hidden action could restore order and coherence to persons, to the world, and to the spirit.

Paul Tillich, though an exile and not a conspirator, was of the conspirators' generation, and his thoughts on the "moral imperative," written a generation after the Second World War, reflect the conspirators' experience.

The "moral imperative," Tillich writes, "is the command to become what one potentially is, a person within a community of persons."[32] Developing his theme, Tillich adds:

> The moral imperative is the demand to become actually what one is essentially and therefore potentially. . . . His true being shall become his actual being—this is the moral imperative. . . . Every moral act is an act in which an individual self establishes itself as a person. . . . Therefore, a moral act is not an act in obedience to an external law. . . . It is the inner law of our true being. . . . And an anti-moral act . . . drives toward disintegration. . . . The voice of man's essential being is silenced . . . [resulting in] . . . a disintegrating self . . . depersonalization . . . the moral act is always a victory over disintegrating forces.[33]

For Tillich, this instinct and capacity for personal integrity, this repugnance for chaos and disintegration, is in a sense preethical and prereligious. It arises in the painful awareness of separation and division: "the self discovers itself in the experi-

ence of a split between what it is and what it ought to be."[34]
Indeed, this awareness of disintegration, what Martin Luther
called the "attacks are the most terrible thing a human being can
experience. They create an incredible Angst . . . a feeling of being
enclosed in a narrow place from which there is no escape."[35] But
this "bad conscience" is a good thing. Tillich cites Nietzsche's
observation that "the bad conscience is a sickness, but it is a
sickness as pregnancy is one."[36] In "After Ten Years," Bonhoeffer
made the same point when he warned that a happy conscience
may indeed be dangerous: "a bad conscience may be stronger
and more wholesome than a deluded one."[37]

The need to escape the trap of chaos, the need to restore integrity, is rooted not only in the psychological need for identity but
in the equally powerful need for love. "Love in all its qualities
drives toward reunion . . . with things and persons in their essential goodness and with good itself," Tillich writes.[38] The ethical
conscience is, therefore, a kind of "transmoral" conscience, in
that it is driven not simply by "law" but by something which is
even before law. "A conscience may be called 'transmoral,'" Tillich writes, "if it judges not in obedience to a moral law, but
according to its participation in a reality that transcends the
sphere of moral commands."[39] And this, Tillich argues, is what
Luther meant by "justification by grace."[40]

This is dangerous business. To be aware of chaos and disintegration means living in a world of chaos and disintegration.
Chaos, disintegration, and finitude are inescapable elements of
our fallen human condition. To overcome them, we must encounter and confront them, which means entanglement with
them. Yet this is the road required by the unconditional call of
grace. Martin Heidegger, Tillich notes, argued that: "The call of
conscience has the character of the demand that man in his finitude actualize his genuine potentialities, and this means an appeal to become guilty." To which Tillich adds:

Conscience summons us to ourselves, calling us back from the talk
of the market and the conventional behavior of the masses. It has no
special demands; it speaks to us in the "mode of silence." It tells
us only to act and to become guilty by acting, for every action is
unscrupulous. He who acts experiences the call of conscience and,
at the same time, has the experience of contradicting his conscience,
of being guilty. "Existence as such is guilty." Only self-deception can
give a good moral conscience, since it is impossible not to act and
since every action implies guilt. We must act, and the attitude in
which we can act is "resoluteness." Resoluteness transcends the

moral conscience . . . the good, transmoral conscience consists in the acceptance of the bad, moral conscience which is unavoidable whenever decisions are made and acts are performed.[41]

The unconditional response to the unconditional call of grace is death. "When Christ calls a person," Bonhoeffer writes, "He calls that person to die."[42] Yet this death in response to grace is not negation, but redemption.

The conspirators thought much about death. They knew that their conspiracy meant killing; they knew that it was likely to fail; they knew that participation in it almost certainly meant their own death. "Fundamentally," Dietrich Bonhoeffer wrote at the conclusion of "After Ten Years,"

> We feel that we really belong to death already, and that every new day is a miracle . . . we should like to see something more of the meaning of our life's broken fragments. . . . We still love life, but I do not think that death can take us by surprise now . . . we should like death to come to us, not accidentally and suddenly through some trivial cause, but in the fullness of life and with everything at stake.[43]

Yet, death "in the fullness of life and with everything at stake" can also be redeeming. It was not merely "risking death" that was redeeming, nor was the redemption possible simply a personal redemption. The conspirators often spoke of atonement and purgation of guilt, but they rarely spoke of their own personal redemption. It was the death itself that was redemptive, and it was redemptive not of individual persons, but of time itself.

One way to understand the conspirators' idea of redemptive death is to borrow Alasdair MacIntyre's notion of "practice."

A "practice," MacIntyre writes, is an unusual form of human action. A "practice" is a kind of collective, cooperative action, based on some notion of an objective standard of excellence. Persons engaged in a "practice" judge their action in part on the extent to which the action accords with "excellence." Excellence, to be sure, can be variously defined; standards of excellence may well vary through time and across space, but nevertheless, what characterizes a "practice" is the conviction that it does make sense to act with some sense of "excellence" in mind, "excellence" which is more than subjective opinion, more than mere "life-style." And because this acting in the shadow of excellence is cooperative and collective, qualities like "justice," "courage," and "honesty," however variously defined, are extremely important.[44]

The 20 July plot was a kind of "practice." The "excellence" which informed the conspirators' actions was their sense of the unconditional call of grace for integrity, and for overcoming chaos, and disintegration. And the sign of their total subordination to this sense of excellence was death.

Yet "subordination" is not entirely accurate. For in dying, the conspirators hoped to bring into reality, as admonition and example, their sense of excellence, their experience of grace. Their deaths would dramatically demonstrate the reality of grace in time; their deaths would demonstrate not simply "subordination" but "incarnation." "Christ calls a person to die," Bonhoeffer thought, so that a person dying in response to grace could share in the incarnation. And this demonstration of the reality of incarnation not only echoed the ancient event of incarnation so central to Christianity, but would serve to demonstrate to the future the possibility, and the reality, of incarnation, of grace becoming real in time.

Dietrich Bonhoeffer was hanged on 9 April 1945. According to one witness, Bonhoeffer's last comment was "For me this is the end, but also the beginning."[45] It may well be that Bonhoeffer was speaking in the traditional religious sense of leaving this sphere of reality and somehow entering "another." Given Bonhoeffer's skepticism about "two-sphere" thought, however, this seems unlikely. Perhaps what Bonhoeffer had in mind in those last seconds of his life was not simply "going to heaven," but participating in the incarnation that was so central to him. His death, while in the attempt to restore integrity to life, was the final and culminating participation in the experience of grace in life, in incarnation.

Finally, the possibility and the reality of incarnation was the source of the conspirators' hope.

The conspirators were persons of hope, not optimism. They had few illusions about human nature, they had little confidence that history would automatically improve, they knew full well the capacity of human beings for evil. They cannot be called optimists.

Optimism, in the sense of human self-confidence, is, as Reinhold Niebuhr writes, both naive and, like despair, contrary to faith.[46] Hope, however, is the firm conviction that the "kingdom of truth" is, and can be, incarnated in time.

"The kingdom, which is not of this world, is always in this world in man's uneasy conscience," Niebuhr wrote just before the outbreak of the war.[47] He adds: "the kingdom of truth constantly enters the world. And its entrance descends beyond conscience into action."[48] "The world," Niebuhr explains,

> . . . is alienated from its true character. . . . The kingdom of truth is consequently not the kingdom of some other world. It is the picture of what this world ought to be. This kingdom is thus not of this world, inasfar as the world is constantly denying the fundamental laws of human existence. Yet it is of this world. It is not some realm of eternal perfection which has nothing to do with historical existence. It constantly impinges upon man's every decision and is involved in every action.[49]

It is this sense of the reality of the kingdom which provided Bonhoeffer, and the conspirators, not with optimism, but with hope. This was a hope inspired, in part, by the revolution in the conspirators' perspective. Concluding "After Ten Years," Bonhoeffer writes:

> There remains an experience of incomparable value. We have for once learnt to see the great events of world history from below, from the perspective of the outcast, the suspects, the maltreated, the powerless, the oppressed, the reviled—in short, from the perspective of those who suffer. The important thing is that neither bitterness nor envy should have gnawed at the heart during this time, that we should have come to look with new eyes at matters great and small, sorrow and joy, strength and weakness, that our perception of generosity, humanity, justice and mercy should have become clearer, freer, less corruptible. We have to learn that personal suffering is a more effective key, a more rewarding principle for exploring the world in thought and action than personal good fortune. This perspective from below must not become the partisan possession of those who are eternally dissatisfied; rather we must do justice to life in all its dimensions from a higher satisfaction, whose foundation is beyond any talk of "from below" or "from above." This is the way in which we may affirm it.[50]

On 21 July 1944, the day after the collapse of the coup, Bonhoeffer wrote, from his prison cell, a brief letter to Eberhard Bethge. Whatever optimism Bonhoeffer may have had about the conspiracy was shattered. Now his life, and lives of everyone implicated in the coup, was forfeit. This is what he wrote to Bethge:

Dear Eberhard,

. . . During the last year or so I've come to know and understand more and more the profound this-worldliness of Christianity. The Christian is not a "homo religiosus," but simply a human being, as Jesus was a human being. . . . I don't mean the shallow and banal this-worldliness of the enlightened, the busy, the comfortable, or the lascivious, but the profound this-worldliness, characterized by discipline and the constant knowledge of death and resurrection. . . .

I remember a conversation that I had in America thirteen years ago with a young French pastor. We were asking ourselves quite simply what we wanted to do with our lives. He said he would like to become a saint (and I think it's quite likely that he did become one). At the time I was very impressed, but I disagreed with him, and said, in effect, that I should like to learn to have faith. For a long time I didn't realize the depth of the contrast. I thought I could acquire faith by trying to live a holy life, or something like it. . . . I discovered later, and I'm still discovering right up to this moment, that it is only by living completely in this world that one learns to have faith. One must completely abandon any attempt to make something of oneself, whether it be a saint, or a converted sinner, or a church official . . . a righteous person or an unrighteous one, a sick person or a healthy one. By this-worldliness I mean living unreservedly in life's duties, problems, successes and failures, experiences and perplexities. In so doing we throw ourselves completely into the arms of God, taking seriously, not our own sufferings, but those of God in the world— watching with Christ in Gethsemane. That, I think, is faith. . . . I'm glad to have been able to learn this, and I know I've been able to do so only along the road that I've travelled. So I'm grateful for the past and present, and content with them. . . .

May God in his mercy lead us through these times; but above all, may he lead us to himself. . . .

Good-bye. Keep well, and don't lose hope that we shall all meet again soon. I always think of you in faithfulness and gratitude.

Yours,
Dietrich[51]

Epitaph: Gewitteraktion

> Thus, choosing to die resisting, rather than to live submitting,
> they fled only from dishonor, met danger face to face, and,
> after one brief moment of terror, while at the height of their
> glory, escaped, not from their fear, but into immortality. And
> so died these men as became Athenians. You, their survivors,
> must determine to behave as they did, though you may pray
> for a happier end.
>
> —Pericles, "Oration on the Athenian Dead"

Friday, 21 July 1944. Order had finally returned to the Wolf's
Lair. Hitler visited those of his staff who had been injured by
Stauffenberg's bomb. Hitler suffered from intense pain in his
right ear, his eyes twitched to the right, and he seemed to have
difficulty keeping his balance, but the doctors assured him that
he had suffered no permanent injury.[1]

On Saturday, 22 July, Hitler met with some of his key advisors
in the Wolf's Lair Teahouse, only a few steps away from the
bombed-out briefing barracks. Keitel, Himmler, Goebbels, Bormann, and Albert Speer attended.

Hitler, Speer recalled, seemed calm at first. But when he spoke
about the assassination attempt, he exploded. "Now I know why
all my great plans in Russia had to fail in recent years!" he
shouted. "It was all treason!" As for the conspirators, Hitler
vowed to "annihilate and exterminate them." Himmler was
charged with tracking down the conspirators, and, after the meeting, Himmler ordered Gestapo chief Ernst Kaltenbrunner to begin the investigation. It was called *Gewitteraktion, Operation
Thunderstorm.*[2]

While Kaltenbrunner launched Thunderstorm, Nazi party and
government leaders took turns denouncing the conspirators.
Heinz Guderian, the Army's new commander, pledged Hitler the
loyalty of the officer corps, and soon the Nazi party greeting
replaced the traditional army salute. On Saturday, 22 July, the

Völkischer Beobachter, the Nazi party paper, carried headlines that proclaimed "The Nation's Answer: Absolute Loyalty"; and "Goering: in True and Fervent Love for the Führer," and so on.[3] Heinrich Himmler vowed to a meeting of Party Gauleiters that the Stauffenberg family would be exterminated root and branch. "Let no one come to us and say: what you are doing is Bolshevistic," Himmler told his audience.

> No . . . it isn't Bolshevistic at all, but a very old custom practiced among our forefathers. . . . When they placed a family under the ban . . . they said: This man has committed treason; the blood is bad; there is traitor's blood in him; that must be wiped out. And in the blood feud, the entire clan was wiped out down to the last member. The family of Count Stauffenberg will be wiped out to the last member.[4]

Robert Ley, the head of the Nazi labor organization, bellowed in an editorial for a party newspaper:

> Degenerate to their very bones, blue-blooded to the point of idiocy, nauseatingly corrupt, and cowardly like all nasty creatures—such is the aristocratic clique which the Jew has sicked on National Socialism. . . . We must exterminate this filth, extirpate it root and branch! . . . It is not enough simply to seize the offensive . . . we must exterminate the entire breed![5]

Top-secret SS intelligence reports contained good news for the führer. According to SS sources, most Germans had reacted unfavorably to the news of the assassination attempt:

> The failed assassination and coup attempt of the officer-clique have forced military news into the background. After recovering from the shock of the assassination itself, people express concern about the background and possible results of this event. . . . People are relieved that the Führer did not fall victim to the assassination attempt. Just about everywhere, loyalty to the Führer had deepened. . . . People cannot understand how the assassination attempt was possible in the first place. They denounce the "string-pullers" in no uncertain terms, and vehemently attack the conspirators in extremely strong terms.[6]

At the Front, soldiers reacted angrily to confusing rumors of plots and assassinations at home. Tension between officers and police increased as the Gestapo tried to ferret out the conspiracy's military sympathizers.[7]

Meanwhile, Kaltenbrunner's Gestapo agents unraveled the plot. They were astounded by its breadth and depth. The best estimate is that by the end of the war, some seven thousand people were arrested and charged with complicity in the plot, though in fact, probably no more than a few hundred of these had actually been active conspirators.

Arrests were remarkably easy to make. Some conspirators, to be sure, like Hans Bernd Gisevius, escaped. Carl Goerdeler remained at large for a few weeks. And there was a wave of suicides in the summer and fall of 1944. Henning von Tresckow killed himself on 21 July. Field Marshal Erwin Rommel, though his involvement in the conspiracy was slight, was permitted by the Gestapo to commit suicide. In general, though, the conspirators calmly waited for the knock on the door. Some were exhausted and apathetic; some seemed relieved that the conspiracy was over. All knew that they were going to their deaths, but few seemed frightened.

As Himmler promised, the families of the accused were arrested as well. Adults were sent to concentration camps; children, their names changed, were distributed among ideologically sound foster families. Christa von Hofacker, for example, was thirteen in 1944. Her father, Cäsar von Hofacker, a Stauffenberg cousin, had led the coup in Paris. He was executed in December 1944. Christa, together with Uta von Tresckow, one of Henning von Tresckow's children, was sent to a family in Munich. Later she recalled:

> They took all my money and all my other things . . . even my pictures of Mom and Dad. . . . We were forbidden to tell anyone our right names. I often thought of father, and how they had tortured him and how brave he was, and that made me brave too.[8]

The first wave of defendants were put on trial in August before Judge Roland Freisler's People's Court (Volksgerichthof). The trials were filmed and the films were carefully edited.

Before a selected audience, Judge Freisler played his part well. Attired in a brilliant red robe, he shouted at the defendants, ridiculed them, and called them every name his febrile imagination could conjure up.

Defendants, exhausted and unkempt, were dressed in ragged old clothes. They looked more like hobos than officers and state officials. A few broke down. The majority stayed calm, though Freisler seldom permitted them a word. Old Field Marshal Erwin von Witzleben was able to shout: "You can hand us over to the executioner but in three months' time this outraged and suffering people will call you to account and drag you alive through the mud of the streets!"[9] Hans Bernd von Haeften, the Foreign Office conspirator, whose brother had died at Stauffenberg's side, was briefly able to explain his actions:

> *Freisler.* So. Don't you see that when a people is in a fight for its life . . . that it is treason to violate your oath to the Führer?
> *Haeften.* I am no longer concerned with this oath.
> *Freisler.* Aha! So now it's clear. You're not concerned about this oath, you're free to commit treason. . . .
> *Haeften.* No, that's not it. From my point of view, I've come to the conclusion that the Führer is the focus of evil in the world and. . . .
> *Freisler.* So! There's nothing more to say.[10]

Helmuth James von Moltke, according to his last letters to his wife, Freya, seemed almost to enjoy sparring with Freisler. During Freisler's tirades, Moltke sat quietly and smiled. Freisler thought it important to point out the significance of the participation of theologians and ministers, like Jesuit father Alfred Delp, in Moltke's Kreisau Circle, and Moltke thoroughly agreed. Not without irony, however. As he wrote to Freya: "That I should die as a martyr for Ignatius Loyola . . . really is comical, and I already tremble at the thought of Papa's paternal indignation, since he was always so anti-Catholic. The rest he would approve, but that!"

It was important to Moltke that his case be distinguished from those of the direct participants in the assassination attempt. He had opposed the idea of assassination from the first—he had always insisted that Germany had to be destroyed utterly if Nazism were to die, and he refused to "save what could be saved." He was quite willing to hang, but he insisted on hanging not because he was an assassin but because he was a resister. Moltke was pleased that Freisler stressed the religious ambience of the Kreisau Circle. As he wrote to his Freya:

> All in all, this emphasis on the religious aspect of the case corresponds with the real inwardness of the matter, and shows that Freisler is, after all, a good judge, from the political angle. This gives us the inestimable advantage of being killed for something which we have really done, and which is worthwhile.[11]

Almost all of the defendants were, of course, sentenced to

death. Most were permitted to write last letters, and many of these have survived.

Ulrich von Hassell wrote to his wife only minutes before his execution:

8 September 1944.
Dearest Ilse,
Thirty years ago today, I was wounded in France. I still carry the bullet with me near my heart. Today, the People's Court handed down its decision. If it is carried out, as I assume it will be, so will end the extraordinary happiness that you have given me. It really was too fine to continue. At this moment, I am filled with the deepest thanks to God and to you. You have stood beside me and given me peace and strength. And this thought outweighs the pain I feel at leaving you and the children. May God permit us to find each other again. You will remain alive, that is my greatest comfort . . . and that you are strong and brave, and will be a pillar, but a dear and kind pillar, for the children. Remain as good and kind as you are, never be bitter. God bless you, and God bless Germany. With all my love.

Hans Bernd von Haeften wrote to his wife, Barbara:

. . . my dearest Barbara . . . in a few hours I will be in God's hands. So, I will say goodbye . . . I die in the assurance of God's forgiveness . . . with the certainty that all the pain . . . that I have caused for you . . . He will turn into blessings . . . dear Barbara, I thank you from the bottom of my heart for all the love and joy you have given me in our fourteen years of marriage. Please forgive my lack of love, I have loved you more than I have been able to say. . . . Kiss the children for me . . . I embrace you and hold you to my heart.

And Peter Yorck von Wartenburg concluded his farewell letter to his wife:

I am dying for my country. Even if the appearance is one of shame, I will take my last steps straight and unbowed, and I hope you will not think this arrogant. We wished to light a fire for life, and a sea of flame overwhelms us.[12]

In ones and twos they were taken to Berlin's Plötzensee prison and killed. Hitler killed them cruelly. He ordered them to be hanged, "strung up like butchered cattle," he said,[13] but he wanted them hanged so that they would die not suddenly of a broken neck, but slowly, by strangulation. The executions were

filmed for Hitler's later entertainment. According to their executioners, the men killed at Plötzensee died well.[14]

Their bodies were given to the Anatomical Institute of Berlin
University. The Institute's director had friends among the conspirators' families, and he refused to use the bodies as cadavers.
He had them cremated instead. An Allied air raid destroyed most
of the urns containing the conspirators' ashes.[15]

The killings slackened after August. The Gestapo decided that
there was no point in killing all of their potential witnesses.
The killings slackened, but did not cease. In fact, the killings
continued to the very last days of the war. People associated with
the Abwehr, Wilhelm Canaris, Hans Oster, Hans von Dohnanyi,
and Dietrich Bonhoeffer, for example, survived until the spring
of 1945. Himmler then ordered them all killed. Dohnanyi was
shot in Berlin. Oster, Canaris, and Bonhoeffer were hanged at
the Flossenburg camp in April 1945. Bonhoeffer, composed to
the end, remarked: "This is the end—for me, it is the beginning
of life."[16] Their bodies were burned and their ashes scattered.

Virtually everyone connected with the conspiracy died before
the end of the war, either at his own hand or at the hands of
executioners: Ludwig Beck, Carl Gordeler, Henning von Tresckow, Wilhelm Canaris, Hans Oster, Hans von Dohnanyi, Dietrich Bonhoeffer, the Haeften brothers, the Stauffenberg brothers.
But not everyone died.

Hans Bernd Gisevius, the conspiracy's man in Zurich, was in
Berlin during the coup, but he managed to escape and make
his way to Switzerland. Although the Stauffenberg family was
arrested, and the Stauffenberg children placed in foster homes,
they all survived the war and were reunited at the war's end.
Freya von Moltke and Marion Yorck von Wartenburg survived as
well. Before she left the Moltke estate in Silesia, Freya Moltke
retrieved Helmuth's notes and papers, which became an invalu-
able source of information about the Kreisau Circle and the 20
July Conspiracy.

Fabian von Schlabrendorff, Henning von Tresckow's aide, was
arrested shortly after Tresckow's suicide. He was beaten so se-
verely that, though only thirty-eight, he suffered a series of heart
attacks. In an effort to terrorize him, the Gestapo took him to
Tresckow's grave, and forced him to watch while they exhumed
Tresckow's body and burned it. In February 1945, Schlabrendorff was brought before Judge Freisler.

Schlabrendorff, exhausted, tried to make his defense. "At the
very beginning," Schlabrendorff wrote later, "I said that two hun-

dred years ago, Frederick the Great had abolished torture in Prussia, but that I had been tortured." He then recounted what he had been through, but it was too much. He broke down and began to cry. As he wept, the courtroom was absolutely still.[17]

An air raid interrupted Schlabrendorff's trial, and when the raid was over, Judge Freisler was dead, buried beneath a heap of rubble.

Freisler's replacement, incredibly, found Schlabrendorff not guilty. The Gestapo were unhappy with the verdict, however, and rearrested Schlabrendorff as he left the courtroom. The Gestapo were not without a sense of propriety though. They informed Schlabrendorff that he would be executed, and then asked him to sign a certificate testifying that he had been so informed.

But Schlabrendorff was not executed. Instead, he became part of a strange little caravan, whose fate marked the end of the conspiracy and the end of the Second World War in Europe.

Schlabrendorff was shipped to Dachau. His papers were lost, and when a Dachau officer asked Schlabrendorff what he was imprisoned for, Schlabrendorff responded simply that he was a "political." Dachau was full of important "politicals," and Schlabrendorff joined them.

At the end of April 1945, as American troops invaded southern Germany, guards hastily rounded by Dachau's "politicals," herded them onto trucks, and carted them off to Austria.

It was a peculiar convoy. The SS drivers and guards had no idea where they were going; they had no idea whether they were to kill their prisoners or hold them hostage. As for the prisoners, they included, besides Fabian von Schlabrendorff, Pastor Martin Niemoeller, the Lutheran minister who had been in concentration camps since 1938; several German generals who had been implicated in the 20 July Conspiracy; Leon Blum, the former Premier of France; a nephew of Soviet Foreign Minister Molotov; a cousin of Winston Churchill; the Bishop of Clermont-Ferrand; Prince Friedrich of Prussia; and Prince Francis-Xavier de Bourbon-Parma—altogether, the prisoners represented some twenty-seven different nationalities.

The little convoy wound its way over the snow-slick roads, ever deeper into the breathtaking Austrian Alps. Finally, in northern Italy, it stopped at a small mountain resort. Prisoners were housed in the resort's rooms. The officers in the convoy persuaded the jittery SS guards to turn the convoy over to a Wehrmacht detachment. The guards agreed. The regular army took command of the convoy. Leon Blum, in his resort room, awoke to find a German army officer, immaculately uniformed as if parading before the old Kaiser, standing before him. The officer clicked his heels, saluted smartly, and informed Monsieur Blum that he and his wife were now safely in the hands of the German army. Blum remarked later: "I had not expected to be liberated from the concentration camps by an officer of the Imperial Germany Army."[18]

And that was the end. The German troops surrendered the prisoners to Americans, who sent them to southern Italy for medical care. When Schlabrendorff told the Americans his story, they urged him to write a complete report, and with that, the 20 July Conspiracy against Hitler ended, and its story began.[19]

And now, what are we to make of them, these conspirators? Joachim Fest, in his biography of Hitler, summarizes the most familiar argument concerning the moral imagination of the 20 July Conspirators:

> ... there remains in all the statements and activities of the German opposition an unmistakable note of deep despair. This evidently sprang not so much from the feeling of powerlessness in the face of the brutal regime as from the inner impotence of people who had recognized the anachronistic, crippling nature of their values, but were nevertheless unable to give those values up ... [they] had to conquer a thousand resistances within themselves before they could resolve to act.

Fest concludes: "None of their ideas and values have come down to the present day. They left scarcely a trace."[20]

On both counts, Fest's argument is wrong. The conspirators did not resist despite who they were but because of who they were. Their inner struggle was not an effort to repudiate their values, but to be true to them.

And what of Fest's other point, that they left nothing behind? It is quite true that the conspiracy was the final act of an old world, an old Germany, not the opening act of a newer world and a newer Germany. The classes and institutions the conspirators represented have all but vanished. Their peculiar blend of hauteur and self-sacrifice, irony and commitment, seem to belong to a much different world. Much is lost but not all. Memory remains.

In William Faulkner's story, "The Bear," a young hound,

trembling and terrified, all alone, works up enough courage to attack a fierce bear. The bear rakes the hound with its claws and hurls it aside. An old Indian later salves the hound's wounds, and as he does so, he ruefully remarks:

> Just like a man . . . just like folks. Put off as long as she could having to be brave, knowing all the time that sooner or later she would have to be brave once so she could keep on calling herself a dog, and knowing beforehand what was going to happen when she done it.[21]

With their mordant sense of humor, the conspirators might not object too much to a comparison with Faulkner's hound. They too put off being brave as long as they could, not wanting to resist, but in the end having to resist just so they could keep on calling themselves human, knowing beforehand full well what their resistance would mean.

The conspirators were indeed heroes, but in a terrible way. It struck them that their circumstances were somehow Aeschylean, Shakespearean, that they had brought much evil on themselves and on their own world—"We learned to lie easily." Dietrich Bonhoeffer prayed in prison, "afraid of suffering and poor in deeds / We have betrayed Thee before men"[22]—yet hoping that through suffering, and through their deaths, they could find wisdom or peace or perhaps redemption. They were not models of virtue but signs of contradiction, caught up in forces they thought they understood but did not, and the only uncompromised virtue left to them was doomed courage.

Later generations are right to criticize them, as they criticized themselves, but later generations should not congratulate themselves too much on their own virtue. The 20 July Conspirators confronted a moral crisis for which they were utterly unprepared, the like of which few generations have had to face. We, their heirs, as Pericles suggested long ago, should pray that we never face such a fate. Even as we pray, however, we should remember C. S. Lewis's admonition:

> . . . little people like you and me, if our prayers are sometimes granted, beyond all hope and probability, had better not draw hasty conclusions to our own advantage. If we were stronger, we might be less tenderly treated. If we were braver, we might be sent, with far less help, to defend more desperate posts in the great battle.[23]

Notes

Prologue: Resistance and Civic Virtue

1. Edmund Burke, *Reflections on the Revolution in France* (New York: Penguin, 1969), 171.
2. H. Stuart Hughes, "Contemporary Historiography: Progress, Paradigms, and the Regression Toward Positivism," cited by Dominick Lacapra in "Letters," *American Historical Review*, Vol. 88, No. 3, June 1983.
3. Theodor Eschenburg, "Das obsolete Ehrenwort," *Die Zeit*, 10 February 1984, 4.
4. "What Ever Happened to Ethics?" *Time*, 24 May 1987, 14–33.
5. Robert Bellah, et al., *Habits of the Heart* (New York: Perennial Library, 1985), vi.
6. See Richard Neuhaus, *The Naked Public Square* (Grand Rapids, Mich.: William Eerdmans, 1984).
7. See Paul Fussell, *The Great War and Modern Memory* (New York: Oxford, 1975). Fussell argues that the Great War created the essentially "ironic" mode that dominates modern consciousness in the West.
8. The best known, but by no means only argument that "narcissism" is the distinctive quality of modern Western life, is in Christopher Lasch, *The Culture of Narcissism* (New York: Norton, 1979). See also Daniel Bell, *The Cultural Contradictions of Capitalism* (New York: Basic Books, 1976).
9. See Richard Sennett, *The Fall of Public Man* (New York: Vintage, 1976). Hannah Arendt's work focuses on much the same point. See especially George Kateb's analysis of Arendt: George Kateb, *Hannah Arendt: Politics, Conscience, and Evil* (Totowa, N.J.: Rowman and Allanheld, 1984).
10. Virginia Woolf, *The Waves* (New York: Harcourt Brace, 1931), 157.
11. See Christopher Lasch, *The Minimal Self* (New York: Norton, 1984).
12. Plato, *Apology*, trans. Hugh Tredennick, in Edith Hamilton and Huntington Cairns, eds., *Plato: The Collected Dialogues* (Princeton, N.J.: Bollingen, 1969), 28c–39b.
13. Cicero, *Selected Works*, trans. M. Grant (New York: Penguin, 1971), 135.
14. Livy, *Ab Urbe Condita*, Praefatio, 10; Tacitus, *Annales*, III, 65.
15. Karl Jaspers cited in James Wilkinson, *The Intellectual Resistance in Europe* (Cambridge: Harvard, 1981), 141.
16. Hans Rothfels, *Deutsche Opposition gegen Hitler* (Frankfurt: Fischer, 1986), 24–25. Rothfels, a conservative historian of Jewish background, fled to the United States in 1939. In 1948, he published the first scholarly analysis of the 20 July Conspiracy, which he revised several times over the years. Rothfels's work remains one of the most important studies of the resistance. See also Hermann Graml's introduction to this edition. Rothfels died in 1976.
17. Peter Hoffman, *Widerstand gegen Hitler* (Munich: Piper, 1979), 14.
18. There are only two studies in the immense literature on 20 July which

attempt an ethical analysis of the conspiracy: Mother Mary Alice Gallin, *Ethical and Religious Factors in the German Resistance to Hitler* (Washington, D.C.: Catholic University, 1955), and Dieter Ehlers, *Technik and Moral einer Verschwörung* (Frankfurt: Athenaum, 1964). While both works are useful, neither satisifies the need for a detailed study of the conspirators' moral universe.

19. Jürgen Schmädeke and Peter Steinback, eds., *Der Widerstand gegen den Nationalsozialismus* (Munich: Piper, 1985), 1155.

20. Marie Vassiltchikov, *Berlin Diaries* (New York: Knopf, 1987), 241.

21. Eberhard Zeller, *The Flame of Freedom* (London: Oswald Wolff, 1967), 380.

22. Michael Balfour, *Helmuth von Moltke* (London: Macmillan, 1972), 96.

23. Burke, *Reflections*, 195.

24. Balfour, *Moltke*, 120.

25. Jan Kott, *Shakespeare our Contemporary* (New York: Doubleday, 1966), 43.

Chapter 1. Valkyrie

1. The definitive account of the events of 20 July 1944 is in Peter Hoffmann, *The History of the German Resistance, 1933–1945* (Cambridge: MIT Press, 1977), a translation of his *Widerstand, Staatsstreich, Attentat* (Munich: Piper, 1969). The texts of these documents are in Hoffman's "Appendix 2."

2. Klaus Finker, *Stauffenberg und der 20. Juli 1944* (Cologne: Pahl-Rugenstein, 1977), 144.

3. Ibid., 133.

4. Joachim Dramarz, *Stauffenberg* (New York: Macmillan, 1967), 154. Eberhard Zeller reports the same incident in *Flame*, 361. The young officer who told the story was Lieutenant Urban Thiersch.

5. Christian Müller, *Oberst i.G. Stauffenberg* (Dusseldorf: Droste, 1971), 255.

6. Müller, *Oberst*, 260; Zeller, *Flame*, 187–88.

7. Finker, *Stauffenberg*, 271.

8. Müller, *Oberst*, 231.

9. Zeller, *Flame*, 432 n. 29.

10. A key participant in the events of that day, Hans Hagan, for instance, recalled that "just in terms of the weather, July 20, 1944, was a very hot day." Hans Hagan, *Zwischen Eid und Befehl: Tatzeugenbericht von den Ereignissen am 20. Juli 1944 in Berlin and "Wolfsschanze"* (Munich: Turmer, 1959), 10.

11. The *New York Times*, Thursday, 20 July 1944, 1; The *London Times*, Thursday, 20 July 1944, 1; *Neue Zuricher Zeitung*, Thursday, 20 July 1944, 1.

12. Finker, *Stauffenberg*, 272–73.

13. Vassiltchikov, *Diaries*, 198.

14. Ibid., 105–18; 189.

15. Peter Hoffmann provides a detailed map of the Wolf's Lair in Hoffmann, *History*, 734–35.

16. Ulrich von Hassell was constantly shocked by Keitel's lack of ability. For example, as early as 17 September 1938, Hassell wrote in his diary: "I was amazed that Keitel would be shocked by England's willingness to march in case of conflict. In our discussions, he proved to be entirely unpolitical, and made the most preposterous comments about the chance of war. . . . Weizsacker

thinks he is too stupid to understand such things" in Ulrich von Hassell, *Die Hassell-Tagebücher,* ed. Friedrich Freiherr Hiller von Gaertringen (Berlin: Siedler, 1988), 51. Hassell's comments about Keitel are consistently unflattering. In Hassell's opinion, Keitel was simply a passive instrument in Hitler's hand.

17. See Harold Deutsch, *Hitler and His Generals* (Minneapolis: University of Minnesota, 1974), 272: "His [Keitel's] underlying insecurity was symbolized by the hasty, somewhat faltering gait that was his trademark."

18. A surprisingly large literature has been devoted to Stauffenberg's bombs. They were British-made chemical time-fuse devises. They consisted primarily of hexogen, with other chemical admixtures. Each weighed about two pounds. With the acid time fuse there were no tell-tale ticking noises. The conspirators had originally obtained bombs of this type from the Abwehr, German Military Intelligence, which was led by fellow conspirators Admiral Wilhelm Canaris and General Hans Oster. It remains unclear just where Stauffenberg obtained these two particular bombs. See Hoffman, *History,* 335–36 and 741; also, Peter Hoffmann, *Hitler's Personal Security* (Cambridge: MIT Press, 1979), 247.

19. Another of the many unclear details about the assassination attempt concerns the actual placement of the briefcase. The briefcase was placed next to the thick table leg away from Hitler; the stout leg partially protected Hitler from the bomb blast. How did the briefcase get on the wrong side of the table leg? Stauffenberg certainly tried to place it as near as possible to Hitler. According to some accounts, Stauffenberg placed the briefcase under the heavy table, next to Hitler, but another officer, after inadvertently kicking it, moved the briefcase to the side of the thick table leg away from Hitler. Peter Hoffmann, on the other hand, argues that Stauffenberg himself probably had no choice but to place the briefcase on the outside of the table leg. See Hoffmann, *History,* 400.

20. This was the unused second bomb. Haeften obviously wanted to be rid of the incriminating explosive. Later, the Gestapo hunted through the woods, and retrieved it.

21. Hitler was leaning over the table when the bomb exploded, and the table protected him. The bomb was on the side of the table leg away from Hitler, and the table leg shielded him too. Had the bomb exploded in an underground bunker, where briefings were usually held, it certainly would have killed Hitler, but that Thursday, the briefing was held in a barracks, above ground, and much of the blast effect dissipated. The blast effect, in any case, was reduced because Stauffenberg had been able to use only one, instead of two, bombs. Still, the minor nature of Hitler's injuries is quite remarkable.

22. Just what happened at the Bendlerstrasse from about 1:00 P.M. to about 3:00 P.M. remains unclear. Most of the people who knew what did happen were dead in a matter of hours. Some writers deny that Fellgiebel ever got through to Bendlerstrasse at all. Others say that he did get through, but that his message was garbled and confused. Peter Hoffmann writes that Fellgiebel did get through and that his report was accurate. Olbricht's decision is also a matter of confusion. Critics charge that he lost his nerve; defenders point out that under the circumstances, he had no choice but to delay. In any case, several precious hours that afternoon were lost.

23. Here, too, there is confusion about the exact sequence of events. Mertz did not issue the actual Valkyrie orders, but he did send out the warning orders, without Olbricht's prior approval. See Hoffmann, *History,* 416.

24. Ibid.

25. Hans Bernd Gisevius recreated the conversation in his memoirs. Gisevius did not participate in the conversation, although he was in the Bendlerstrasse later in the afternoon, and his recreation of the conversation is credible. See Hans Bernd Gisevius, *Bis zum bitteren Ende* (Frankfurt: Knaur, 1982), 377.

26. Unlucky Fromm survived his arrest, but was later arrested by the Nazis, and executed, for allowing the conspiracy to hatch within his command. Fabian von Schlabrendorff met him when they were both in prison in Berlin. This conversation is based on Schlabrendorff's account. See Fabian von Schlabrendorff, *Offiziere gegen Hitler* (Berlin: Siedler, 1984), 124. Gisevius's account is virtually identical. See Gisevius, *Ende*, 378.

27. Gisevius, *Ende*, 390.

28. Hagan, *Zwischen*, 23–24; for the official Gestapo report on Remer's activities, see Karl-Heinrich Peter, ed., *Spiegelbild einer Verschwörung* (Stuttgart: Seewald, 1961), 633–43.

29. For Beck's activities, see Nicholas Reynolds, *Beck. Gehorsam und Widerstand* (Munich: Heyne, 1983), 242–43. This is the German translation of Reynold's *Treason Was No Crime* (London: William Kimber, 1979).

30. Gisevius, *Ende*, 286.

31. Gisevius, *Ende*, 395–96; Hoffmann, *History*, 497–98.

32. Rudolf Lill and Heinrich Oberreuter, ed., *20. Juli. Portraits des Widerstands* (Düsseldorf: Econ, 1984), 220. This report comes from Olbricht's son-in-law, Friedrich Georgi.

33. For accounts of the last moments in the Bendlerstrasse, see Gisevius, *Ende*, 409–12; Schlabrendorff, *Offiziere*, 127–28; Hoffmann, *History*, 507–8.

34. Zeller, *Flame*, 101.

35. The text of Hitler's address can be found in Herbert Michaelis, et al., eds., *Ursachen und Folgen: Vom deutschen Zusammenbruch 1918 und 1945 bis zur staatlichen Neuordnung Deutschlands in der Gegenwart* (Berlin: Wendler, 1963), Vol. 21, 488.

36. Hoffmann, *History*, 511. There is some confusion about the cemetery, although, as Hoffmann argues, it was almost certainly the Matthäikirche cemetery in Berlin's Schöneberg district.

Chapter 2. Vermächtnis

1. Hans Karl Fritzsche, *Ein Leben im Schatten des Verrates* (Freiburg: Herder, 1984), 81. Kunrat von Hammerstein is the person who recalled Schulenburg's comment. See Klaus Finker, *Stauffenberg*, 341.

2. Zeller, *Flame*, 126.

3. Ibid., 418–19. Colonel Friedrich Georgi is the source of the citation.

4. Forschungsgemeinschaft 20. Juli, *Bibliographie "Widerstand"* (Munich: Saur, 1984), compiled by Ulrich Cartarius, introduction by Karl Otmar Freiherr von Aretin. Critics charge, with reason, that this concentration on 20 July distracts from the many other forms of resistance that existed in Germany; critics charge that 20 July has incorrectly become identified as *the* German resistance. Unfortunately, such a misleading identification is implied in, for example, the English title of Peter Hoffmann's exhaustive study of the 20 July Conspiracy. Hoffmann's German title is *Widerstand, Staatsstreich, Attentat* ("Resistance, Coup, and Assassination"). The English title, however, is *The German Resistance to Hitler*.

5. The phrase "broken its teeth" is from Antonio Machado, who writes in another context: "the 'other' refused to disappear; it subsists; it persists; it is the hard bone on which reason breaks its teeth" cited in Octavio Paz, *The Labyrinth of Solitude* (New York: Grove, 1985), 1.

6. For an introduction to the debate about the conspiracy, see, for example, *Bekenntnis and Verpflichtung: Reden und Aufsätze zur zehnjahrigen Wiederkehr des 20. Juli 1944* (Stuttgart: Friedrich Vorwerk, 1955), and in particular, the essay by Hans Rothfels, "Zum politischen Vermächtnis des deutschen Widerstands," 60–83.

7. Friedrich Reck-Malleczewin, *Diary of a Man in Despair* (New York: Macmillan, 1970), 195–98.

8. Otto John, *"Falsch und zu Spät"* (Frankfurt/Main: Ullstein, 1989), 163.

9. "Hitler Hangs his Generals," *New York Times*, 9 August 1944, 16.

10. "International Swine," *New York Herald Tribune*, 9 August 1944, 12.

11. Finker, *Stauffenberg*, 9.

12. Ibid., 366.

13. Ibid., 367.

14. Hans Rothfels, *The German Opposition to Hitler* (Hinsdale: Regnery, 1948); the most recent edition of this work is entitled, *Die Deutsche Opposition gegen Hitler* (Frankfurt: Fischer, 1986). See also Allen Dulles, *Germany's Underground* (New York: Macmillan, 1947). As an OSS officer in Switzerland during the war, Dulles was in close contact with representatives of the German resistance.

15. Countess Marion Dönhoff, "In Memoriam 20. Juli." Written in 1945 and privately circulated at first, this essay was one of the earliest attempts to make sense of the conspiracy. Reprinted many times, it can be found in Rüdiger von Voss, ed., *Der 20. Juli 1944* (Augsburg: Neske, 1984), 37–57.

16. Kurt Tauber, *Beyond Eagle and Swastika: German Nationalism Since 1945* (Middletown, Conn.: Wesleyan University Press, 1967), 87. Tauber adds: "The Twentieth of July has assumed enormous importance in the postwar period. . . . It has become the moral justification for the political reconstruction of West Germany . . . the . . . conspiracy [has] assuaged the gnawing guilt of thousands who also had regarded the Nazi regime with growing distrust and resentment, yet dared not to act. The Twentieth of July has provided the lukewarm, the hesitant, the fearful, and the opportunistic of yesterday with a cloak of self-respect" (263–64).

17. Claus Donate, *Deutscher Widerstand gegen den Nationalsozialismus aus der Sicht der Bundeswehr* (Freiburg: Inaugural Dissertation, 1976), 140.

18. For a discussion of German resistance and pedagogy, see Hans-Jochen Markmann, *Der deutsche Widerstand gegen den Nationalsozialismus, 1933–1945. Modelle für den Unterricht* (Mainz: Hase und Koehler, 1984).

19. Tauber, *Beyond*, 1127.

20. Otto Ernst Remer, *Verschwörung und Verrat um Hitler* (Preussisch Oldendorf: K. W. Schutz, 1984), 7.

21. Remer, *Verschwörung*, 10. Remer organized a neo-Nazi group called the "Sozialistische Reichspartei" in the early 1950s, and made a career out of attacking the July 20 Conspirators. He was periodically sued for libel, for example, in Braunschweig in 1952; he engaged in a long fight with the West German government over his military pension (by the end of the war, he was a general), and over his alleged failure to pay his income tax. There were also allegations that Remer was involved in black market deals with anti-Israeli groups in the Middle East.

For more on Remer see Tauber, *Beyond*, 264, 1285; Markmann, *Widerstand*, 174; Hermann Graml, et al., *The German Resistance to Hitler* (Berkeley: University of California Press, 1970), 195, the English translation of Hermann Graml, ed., *Widerstand im Dritten Reich* (Frankfurt: Fischer, 1984); "Heroes or Traitors?" *Time*, 24 March 1952, 52; *New York Times*, 18 May 1963, 2.

22. Hagen, *Zwischen*, 82–83.

23. Finker, *Stauffenberg*, 280.

24. For a detailed critique of the "legend," see Hans-Peter Rouette, *Die Widerstandslegende* (Berlin: Inaugural Dissertation, Freie University of Berlin, 1983).

25. The term, taken from another context, is C. Vann Woodward's; see C. Vann Woodward, *Thinking Back* (Baton Rouge: Louisiana University, 1986), 4.

26. Hannah Arendt, *Eichmann in Jerusalem* (New York: Vintage, 1963), 97–105. Although Arendt recognizes the bravery of individual conspirators, she is little impressed by the conservative conspiracy in general, and cites with approval Friedrich Reck-Malleczwen's observation that the conspirators were simply trying to establish a "political alibi."

27. Finker, *Stauffenberg*, 9.

28. Ralf Dahrendorf, *Society and Democracy in Germany* (New York: Doubleday, 1967), 391.

29. Hermann Graml, ed., *Widerstand im Dritten Reich* (Frankfurt: Fischer, 1984).

30. Klaus-Jürgen Müller, *Armee, Politik, und Gesellschaft in Deutschland, 1933–1945* (Paderborn: Schöningh, 1979), 9.

31. See Aretin's introduction to Ulrich Cartarius, *Deutscher Widerstand* (Berlin: Siedler, 1984), 7; Forschungsgemeinschaft 20. Juli, *Bibliographie*, 11. For the other perspective, which does draw a clear line from the values of the July 20 Conspirators to the Bonn Republic, see Hans Rothfels, "Gegen die Anmassung des Totalitären," in Pitt Severin and Hartmut Jetter, ed., *25 Jahre Bundesrepublik Deutschland* (Munich: Fritz Molden, 1974), 111, and the remarks of Eberhard Diepgen, Berlin's mayor in 1985, in Schmadecke and Steinbach, *Widerstand*, v.

32. Ger van Roon, for example, in his survey of German Resistance, *Widerstand im Dritten Reich* (Munich: Beck, 1981), devotes only three of his twelve chapters to the July 20 Conspiracy; the rest of his study examines the many other forms of resistance. Van Roon argues, in fact, that "from the workers' movement . . . came not only the first resisters. From the workers' movement came the majority of resisters and resistance groups, as local and regional studies demonstrate" (76). Hans-Jochen Markmann's discussion of ways to teach about the resistance, in Markmann, *Widerstand*, is a good example of the increasingly sociological, rather than ethical, approach to the history of the resistance.

33. See Mayor Diepgen's comments in Schmädecke and Steinbach, *Widerstand*, vi.

34. "Feldmarschall Rommel: Das Ende einer Legende," *Der Spiegel*, 21 August 1978. For information about the Filbinger Affair, see *Der Spiegel's* coverage of 10 July 1978. In the last months of World War II, thousands of German soldiers and sailors deserted. Filbinger was a navy prosecutor and was allegedly responsible for some forty-one sentences of execution. Filbinger, after the war, became a leading conservative politician, insisted that he had really been an anti-Nazi at heart, and was elected minister-president of Baden-Württemberg.

When accusations about his wartime actions first circulated, Filbinger denied everything, then modified his denials, then acknowledged them and tried, lamely, to defend them.

35. On the controversy, see "Schwamm drüber kann es nicht geben," *Der Spiegel*, 28 August 1978, 38; "Warum Wehner in Berlin nicht zum 20. Juli Spricht," *Die Welt*, 20 July 1978, 4; Markmann, *Widerstand*, 193.

36. Markmann, *Widerstand*, 123.

37. *Neues Deutschland*, 20 July 1978.

38. "Misplaced Gratitude," *The New Republic*, 13 and 20 August 1984, 8.

39 For a review of the Bitburg Cemetery affair, see Geoffrey Hartman, ed., *Bitburg in Moral and Political Perspective* (Bloomington: University of Indiana Press, 1986).

40. Cited in Ralph Giordano, *Die zweite Schuld oder Von der Last Deutscher zu Sein* (Hamburg: Knaur, 1990), 78.

41. Giordano, *Schuld*, 83. Jorg Friedrich is a student of West German trials of former Nazi officials.

42. Hassell, *Tagebücher*, Introduction, 37.

43. Ger Van Roon, *Neuordnung im Widerstand* (Munich: Oldenbourg, 1967), 152.

44. Zeller, *Flame*, 73.

45. Dietrich Bonhoeffer, *Ethics*, trans. Neville Horton Smith (New York: Macmillan, 1955), 64. This is the translation of Dietrich Bonhoeffer, *Ethik* (Munich: Kaiser, 1949).

Chapter 3. Charakter

1. Bodo Scheurig, *Henning von Tresckow* (Frankfurt: Ullstein, 1980), 154.

2. Marion Yorck von Wartenburg, *Die Stärke der Stille* (Cologne: Eugen Diederich, 1984), 18.

3. Yorck, *Stärke*, 25.

4. A remark of Emmi Bonhoeffer, Dietrich's sister-in-law, in Wolf-Dieter Zimmermann and Ronald Smith, eds., *I Knew Dietrich Bonhoeffer* (New York: Harper & Row, 1966), 35.

5. Albricht Schonherr, in Zimmermann, *I Knew*, 128.

6. Wilhelm Rott, in Zimmermann, *I Knew*, 132.

7. Wolf-Dieter Zimmermann, in Zimmermann, *I Knew*, 62.

8. Eberhart Bethge, *Dietrich Bonhoeffer* (Munich: Kaiser, 1983), 20.

9. Otto Dudzus, in Zimmermann, *I Knew*, 82.

10. Helmut Traub, in Zimmermann, *I Knew*, 157.

11. Balfour, *Moltke*, 63.

12. K. Bausch, in Finker, *Stauffenberg*, 179.

13. The terms are those of Francis Fergusson. See Francis Fergusson, *The Idea of a Theater* (Princeton: Princeton University Press, 1949), 10–14.

14. Bonhoeffer, *Ethics*, 21.

15. Zeller, *Flame*, 127–28.

16. Müller, *Oberst*, 141.

17. Paul Lehmann, in Zimmermann, *I Knew*, 43.

18. See, for example, the comments about Claus Stauffenberg in Joachim Kramarz, *Stauffenberg* (New York: Macmillan, 1967), 59; Ilse von Hassell's comments about her husband, Ulrich, in Hassell, *Tagebücher*, 173; and Bethge's remarks about Bonhoeffer, in Bethge, *Bonhoeffer*, 41.

19. Zeller, *Flame*, 97, 108–9, 112. For a biography of Adam Trott, see Christopher Sykes, *Tormented Loyalty* (New York: Harper & Row, 1969).

20. Scheurig, *Tresckow*, 111; Zeller, *Flame*, 148.

21. Scheurig, *Tresckow*, 33.

22. Ibid., 148.

23. Finker, *Stauffenberg*, 73.

24. Zeller, *Flame*, 126–27.

25. Müller, *Oberst*, 141.

26. Zeller, *Flame*, 289.

27. Ibid., 112.

28. Balfour, *Moltke*, 45.

29. Ibid., 312.

30. Roon, *Neuordnung*, 86.

31. Finker, *Stauffenberg*, 130.

32. Bethge, *Bonhoeffer*, 427.

33. Bonhoeffer, *Ethics*, 45.

34. Zeller, *Flame*, 59.

35. Schlabrendorff, *Offiziere*, 77 ff.

36. Vassiltchikov, *Diaries*, entries for 12 July 1940; 8 August 1940; 18 December 1940; 22 April 1941.

37. Bethge, *Bonhoeffer*, 227.

38. Finker, *Stauffenberg*, 39–40.

39. Zeller, *Flame*, 199.

40. One might begin an inquiry into this tradition by investigating the enormous influence neoclassical thought had on German culture; the key study to consult is E. M. Butler, *The Tyranny of Greece over Germany* (Boston: Beacon, 1935).

41. Eike Middell, *Friedrich Schiller* (Leipzig: Reclam, 1980), 353; also T. J. Reed, *The Classical Center. Goethe and Weimar, 1775–1832* (Totowa, N.J.: Croom Helm, 1980), 144–45.

42. Müller, *Oberst*, 95.

43. Scheurig, *Tresckow*, 113.

44. Bethge writes of Bonhoeffer: "his students noted a surprisingly intense willingness on his part to be available to them." Bethge, *Bonhoeffer*, 481.

45. For a discussion of the significance of this distinction, see Bellah, *Habits*, 66.

46. Wilkenson, *Resistance*, 250.

47. Schlabrendorff, *Offiziere*, 109.

48. Schlabrendorff, *Offiziere*, 129.

49. See Garry Wills, *Cinncinatus* (New York: Doubleday, 1984); Bertram Wyatt-Brown, *Southern Honor* (New York: Oxford, 1982); Philip Mason, *The English Gentleman* (New York: Morrow, 1982); Mark Girouard, *The Return to Camelot. Chivalry and the English Gentleman* (New Haven: Yale University Press, 1981); David Castronovo, *The English Gentleman* (New York: Ungar, 1987).

50. Wolfgang Foerster, *Generaloberst Ludwig Beck* (Munich: Isar, 1953), 155.

51. James Green and John Dolan, eds., *The Essential Thomas More* (New York: New American Library, 1967), 15.

Chapter 4. Vettern

1. Bethge, *Bonhoeffer*, 30.

2. Ibid., 40 ff.

3. Ibid., 34.

4. Zimmermann, *I Knew*, 46–47.

5. Robert Wohl, *The Generation of 1914* (Cambridge: Harvard, 1979). Many historians argue that the fierce clash between generations, and between fathers and sons, which was so typical of Germany in the early twentieth century, is one key to understanding the rise of German fascism. The war between fathers and sons is central to Peter Gay's discussion of Weimer Germany. See Peter Gay, *Weimar Culture* (New York: Harper & Row, 1968). George Mosse sees the Youth Movement as integral to the "crisis of Germany ideology," see George Mosse, *The Crisis of German Ideology* (New York: Grosset & Dunlap, 1964); see also Peter Lowenberg's classic study of young men who grew up during World War I: Peter Lowenberg, "The Psychohistorical Origins of the Nazi Youth Cohort," *American Historical Review*, 76, No. 5, December 1971.

6. Foerster, *Beck*, 9.

7. Ibid., 11.

8. Zimmermann, *I Knew*, 21.

9. Ibid., 22.

10. Ibid., 21.

11. Ibid., 36–37.

12. Roon, *Neuordnung*, 58.

13. Gerhard Ritter, *The German Resistance* (New York: Praeger, 1958), 17.

14. Finker, *Stauffenberg*, 13.

15. See Balfour, *Moltke*, 21, 229.

16. Finker, *Stauffenberg*, 20.

17. Scheurig, *Tresckow*, 13.

18. Balfour, *Moltke*, 182.

19. Dietrich Bonhoeffer, *Letters and Papers from Prison*, trans. Reginald Fuller, et al. (New York: Macmillan, 1971), 7. This is the English translation of *Widerstand und Ergebung: Briefe und Aufzeichnungen aus der Haft* (Munich: Kaiser, 1970). Citations follow the translation, although in some cases, I have amended the translation based on the original German.

20. Finker, *Stauffenberg*, 145; also, 136.

21. See, for example, Simone Weil, *L'Enracinement* (Paris: Gallimard, 1949). The work of Martin Heidegger, Karl Jaspers, Hannah Arendt, and many others, of course, echoes this concern with alienation, estrangement, and the inability of modern women and men to be "at home" in the world.

22. Lieutenant Colonel Tafel; see Balfour, *Moltke*, 96.

23. Bethge outlines Bonhoeffer's family tree in *Bonhoeffer*, 23–34.

24. For a brief portrait of Ruth von Kleist, see Bethge, *Bonhoeffer*, 502–3.

25. Schlabrendorff, *Offiziere*, 10, 144.

26. Ibid., 10–11.

27. Bethge, *Bonhoeffer*, 27.

28. For more on Trotha, see Roon, *Neuordnung*, 94 ff.

29. Balfour, *Moltke*, 110.

30. Roon provides much information about Peter Yorck in *Neuordnung*; Balfour does as well, in *Moltke*. See also the biographical sketch in Lill, *20 Juli*, 363 ff., and throughout Marion Yorck's memoir, *Stärke*.

31. Müller, *Oberst*, 22 ff.

32. Finker, *Stauffenberg*, 180.

33. Deutsch, *Generals*, 289.

34. Yorck, *Stärke*, 60.

35. J. P. Stern, *The Führer and the People* (Berkeley: University of California

Press, 1975), 136. The *Almanach de Gotha* was, of course, the "who's who" of the aristocracy. See also Sebastian Haffner's remarks in his *The Meaning of Hitler* (Cambridge: Harvard, 1983), 59.

36. Joachim Fest, *Hitler*, trans. Richard and Clara Winston (New York: Vintage, 1975), 976–77.

37. Finker, *Stauffenberg*, 230.

38. Graml, *Resistance*, 62, also 116.

39. For a careful discussion of the relationship between money, elite status, and anti-Semitism, see, for example, Fritz Stern, *Gold and Iron* (New York: Knopf, 1977), which examines the relationship between Otto von Bismarck and Gerson von Bleichroder, his Jewish banker.

40. The term "deep play" is Clifford Geertz's. See his well-known essay, "Deep Play: Notes on the Balinese Cockfight," in Clifford Geertz, *The Interpretation of Cultures* (New York: Harper, 1973), 412ff.

41. Sennett, *Fall*, 266.

42. Johannes Huizinga, *Homo Ludens* (Boston: Beacon, 1950), 13. For more on the social importance of play, see Lasch, *Narcissism*, especially 100–125; and Norbert Elias, *The Civilizing Process* (New York: Urizon, 1978), especially vol. 1, chapter 2.

43. The most convenient reprint of the translated script of the film can be found in Maynard Mack, et al., eds., *The Norton Anthology of World Literature*, vol. 2 (New York: Norton, 1984).

44. Bella Fromm, *Blood and Banquets* (New York: Harper & Brothers, 1942), 39, 55–56, 43.

45. Deutsch, *Generals*, 29.

46. Arthur Koestler, *Darkness at Noon* (New York: Bantam, 1968), 174.

47. Joseph Goebbels, *The Goebbels Diaries*, trans. Fred Taylor (New York: Penguin, 1984), 70.

48. Foerster, *Beck*, 145.

49. Remer, *Verschwörung*, 42.

50. Vassiltchikov, *Diaries*, 34.

51. Hassell, *Tagebücher*, 49–53, 53–54, 129–30.

52. Deutsch, *Generals*, 23.

53. Cartarius, *Widerstand*, 13.

54. Fromm, *Blood*, 62.

55. Müller, *Oberst*, 134.

56. Reynolds, *Treason*, 213.

57. Bonhoeffer, *Letters*, 13.

58. See, for example, William S. Allen's comments in his *The Nazi Seizure of Power* (New York: Watts, 1984), 218–32.

59. Schlabrendorff, *Offiziere*, 37.

Chapter 5. Ehre

1. Deutsch, *Generals*, 311.

2. Finker, *Stauffenberg*, 141.

3. Fritzsche, *Leben*, 66. The speaker was General Rost, later killed in action in Italy.

4. Gisevius, *Ende*, 386.

5. The text of the speech can be found in Klaus-Jürgen Müller, *General*

Ludwig Beck. Studien und Dokumente zur politisch-militarischen Vorstllungs-welt und Tätigkeit des Generalstabschefs des deutschen Heeres 1933–1938 (Boppard: Militärgeschichtliches Forschungsamt, 1980), "Ansprache Becks aus Anlass der 125-Jahr-Feier der Kreigsakademie in Berlin," 477–86. It is also discussed by Foerster, *Beck,* 44 ff.

6. These terms, as well as '"community of memory," used below, are discussed in Bellah, et al., *Habits,* 66, 157, 201, and passim.

7. Bethge, *Bonhoeffer,* 494.

8. Foerster, *Beck,* 42.

9. Foerster, *Beck,* 67.

10. Lill, *20. Juli,* 73.

11. Foerster, *Beck,* 14.

12. Ibid., 49.

13. Reynolds, *Treason,* 48.

14. Zeller, *Flame,* 313.

15. Scheurig, *Tresckow,* 134.

16. Roland Barthes, *Mythologies* (New York: Hill & Wang, 1972), 72.

17. Müller, *Oberst,* 79.

18. For more on Fontane, see Ekkhard Verchau, *Theodor Fontane* (Frankfurt: Ullstein, 1983); Joachim Remak, *The Gentle Critic* (Syracuse, N.Y.: Syracuse University Press, 1964). Also Ernest Bramstead, *Aristocracy and the Middle Classes in Germany* (Chicago: University of Chicago Press, 1964), especially 256–68.

19. Romedio Galeazzo von Thun-Hohenstein, *Der Verschwörer* (Berlin: Severin and Siedler, 1982), 40.

20. Deutsch, *Generals,* 124–25.

21. There is a vast literature on this problem. The classic studies are Gerhard Ritter, *The Sword and the Scepter,* trans. Heinz Norden (Coral Gables, Fla.: University of Miami Press, 1969), originally published as *Staatskunst and Kriegshandwerk* (Munich: Oldenbourg, 1954); and Gordon Craig, *The Politics of the Prussian Army* (New York: Oxford, 1972).

22. Hans von Seeckt, *Antikes Feldherrntum* (Berlin, 1929), 63–64.

23. German tactical doctrine insisted on small-unit aggressiveness. German officers were masters at seizing the initiative, they were expert at harassment and infiltration, and they were remarkably skilled at rapidly creating effective task forces out of heterogeneous units. German military success during the war was due primarily to tactics and strategy, not material superiority. See, for example, the discussions in Charles MacDonald, *The Battle of the Huertgen Forest* (New York: Jove, 1963), 23; Max Hastings, *Operation Overlord* (New York: Simon & Schuster, 1984). According to Hastings, "Throughout the Second World War, wherever British or American troops met the Germans on anything like equal strength, the Germans prevailed," 24.

24. Seeckt, *Feldherrntum,* 116. The standard studies of the German army during the Weimar period are F. L. Carsten, *The Reichswehr and Politics* (Berkeley: University of California Press, 1966), and Harold Gordon, *The Reichswehr and the German Republic* (Princeton: Princeton University Press, 1957).

25. Christopher Duffy, *The Military Life of Frederick the Great* (New York: Atheneum, 1985), 334.

26. Donate, *Widerstand,* 28–29.

27. B. H. Liddell Hart, *The German Generals Talk* (New York: Quill, 1948), 22.

28. Ibid., 18.

29. Deutsch, *Generals*, 212.

30. Finker, *Stauffenberg*, 94.

31. Karl Demeter, *The German Officer Corps* (New York: Praeger, 1965), 72. This is the translation of Demeter's *Das Deutsche Offizierkorps in Gesellschaft und Staat* (Frankfurt: Graefe, 1962).

32. Craig, *Politics*, 180, 208, and especially chapter 6, "The State within the State," 217–54. Also Demeter, *Corps*, 80 ff.

33. Demeter, *Corps*, 136. For more on dueling, see also 116 ff. The most detailed discussion of the duel can be found in Ute Frevert, *Ehrenmänner: Das Duell in der bürgerlichen Gesellschaft* (Munich: Beck, 1991).

34. Duffy, *Life*, 334.

35. The distinction is Karl Demeter's. See Demeter, *Corps*, 116–17.

36. The essay is printed in Demeter, *Corps*, 257 ff.

37. "Introductory Order by Wilhelm I to the Ordinance on Tribunals of Honor," 2 May 1874, reprinted in Demeter, *Corps*, 313 ff.

38. Finker, *Stauffenberg*, 40.

39. Müller, *Oberst*, 65.

40. Beck's involvement in the 1934 purge is a matter of some debate. The SS carried out the purge, but the army cooperated with the SS, and Beck, as chief of staff, certainly had some idea of what the SS had in mind. Even if he was not fully informed of the details of the purge, he almost certainly agreed with its outcome. See, for example, Peter Hoffmann's discussion of the matter in *Widerstand gegen Hitler*, 26. On the other hand, Beck's friend and biographer, Wolfgang Foerster, argues that Beck was shocked by the murders which occurred. See Foerster, *Beck*, 53.

41. Müller, *Oberst*, 134.

42. Reynolds, *Treason*, 54.

43. Gerhard Ritter, *Carl Goerdeler und die deutsche Widerstandsbewegung* (Stuttgart: Deutsche Verlagsanstalt, 1984), 411 ff.

44. Deutsch, *Generals*, 21.

45. Schlabrendorff, *Offiziere*, 31.

46. Deutsch, *Generals*, 394.

47. The complete text can be found in Müller, *Beck*, Document 50, 551.

48. Foerster, *Beck*, 143.

49. Roon, *Neuordnung*, 286.

50. Foerster, *Beck*, 89.

51. For example, see Scheurig, *Tresckow*, 115–16; Schlabrendorff, *Offiziere*, 170; Cartarius, *Widerstand*, 148–49.

52. Carl Zuckmayer, *Des Teufels General, Gesammelte Werke*, volume 3 (Frankfurt: Fischer, 1960), 571.

53. Finker, *Stauffenberg*, 170–71.

54. Zeller, *Flame*, 157; Scheurig, *Tresckow*, 103.

55. Balfour, *Moltke*, 171–72.

56. Schlabrendorff, *Offiziere*, 25.

57. Zeller, *Flame*, 39.

58. Finker, *Stauffenberg*, 286.

59. Fritzsche, *Leben*, 72.

60. Hassell, *Tagebücher* 149.

61. Deutsch, *Hitler*, 414.

62. Müller, *Oberst*, 216.

63. Hassell, *Tagebücher*, 360.
64. Liddell Hart, *Generals*, ix.
65. Demeter, *Corps*, 152.
66. Zuckmayer, *General*, 512.
67. Kramarz, *Stauffenberg*, 173.
68. Zeller, *Flame*, 190–91.
69. Kramarz, *Stauffenberg*, 121.
70. Zeller, *Flame*, 183.
71. Scheurig, *Tresckow*, 182.
72. Zeller, *Flame*, 159.
73. Scheurig, *Tresckow*, 187.
74. Fritzsche, *Leben*, 67.

Chapter 6. Anti-Christ

1. Reck-Malleczewen, *Diary*, April 1939, 72–76.
2. Gisevius, *Ende*, 30.
3. Jacques Delarue, *The Gestapo* (New York: Dell, 1964), 57–58.
4. Ernst Fraenkel, *The Dual State* (New York: Octagon, 1969), 107–15.
5. For more on the structure of the Nazi State, see, for example, Robert Koehl, "Feudal Aspects of National Socialism," and T. W. Mason, "The Primacy of Politics—Politics and Economics in National Socialist Germany," both in Henry A. Turner, ed., *Nazism and the Third Reich* (New York: Quadrangle, 1972); also Sebastian Haffner, *Hitler*, 43: "[Hitler] deliberately destroyed the state's ability to function in favor of his personal omnipotence and irreplaceability."
6. Gisevius, *Ende*, 185.
7. Jeremy Noakes and Geoffrey Pridham, *Documents on Hazism* (New York: Viking, 1974), 251. The comments are in "Report of the Regierungsprasident of Hannover to the Reich and Prussian Minister of the Interior, 5 February 1935, concerning the NSDAP and its organizations."
8. See especially Mason, "Politics . . ." in Turner, *Nazism*.
9. For an introduction to the enormous literature concerning the political plans of the 20 July Conspirators, see Graml, *Widerstand*; Rothfels, *Opposition*; Roon, *Ordnung*; Lowenthal, *Widerstand*; Lill, *20. Juli*.
10. There is more than a little truth in Remer's bitter comment about the conspirators' sensibilities: "These people weren't bothered in the least when, in those revolutionary times, Stormtrooper leaders were put up against the wall. What shocked them was when this happened to General von Schliecher and . . . Edgar Jung—they belonged to their 'elite' circle." Remer, *Verschwörung*, 69.
11. Foerster, *Beck*, 53.
12. Ibid., 113.
13. Zeller, *Flame*, 150.
14. Kramarz, *Stauffenberg*, 91.
15. Louis Lochner, ed., *The Goebbels Diaries, 1942–1943* (New York: Doubleday, 1984), 13.
16. Fromm, *Blood*, 1.
17. Wilkinson, *Resistance*, 127.
18. Balfour, *Moltke*, 143.

19. Bonhoeffer, *Letters*, 146.

20. Ibid., 156.

21. Clement Greenberg, "Avant-Garde and Kitsch," in Clement Greenburg, *Art and Culture: Critical Essays* (Boston: Beacon, 1961), 9–10.

22. Ibid., 19.

23. See Saul Friedlander, *Reflections of Nazism: An Essay on Kitsch and Death* (New York: Harper and Row, 1982).

24. Karl Barth, *The Epistle to the Romans* (New York: Oxford, 1977), 53. Barth is commenting on Romans 1:25 – 27.

25. Yorck, *Stärke*, 38.

26. Gisevius, *Ende*, 112.

27. In the summer of 1927, Theodor Haubach, Carlo Mierendorff, and Helmuth von Moltke visited Zuckmayer at his home outside Salzburg. All three later became members of the Kreisau Circle. Zuckmayer wrote later: "The three socialists as it happened were keenly interested in the ideas of English neoconservatism. During the conversations that night, the groundwork was laid for what was later to be the Kreisau Circle." Carl Zuckmayer, *A Part of Myself* (New York: Harcourt Brace Jovanovich, 1966), 42.

28. Zuckmayer, *Part*, 50.

29. Paul Ricoeur, *The Symbolism of Evil* (Boston: Beacon, 1967), 30–32.

30. Georges Bernanos, *Les Grands cimetières sous la lune* (Paris: Plon, 1938), 107.

31. Francis Fergusson, *The Idea of a Theater* (Princeton: Princeton University Press, 1949), 135.

32. Zeller, *Flame*, 393.

33. Bonhoeffer, *Ethics*, 65.

34. Hassell, *Tagebücher*, 132, for 17 October 1939.

35. Zeller, *Flame*, 49–50. Goerdeler, to be sure, remained convinced that if only given the opportunity, he could persuade Hitler to reform the state.

36. See Friedlander's comments on this issue in *Reflections*, 114. The phrase regarding the translation of Hitler into a "metaphysical principle," cited by Friedlander, is Hyam Maccody's.

37. Wilkenson, *Resistance*, 264.

38. Schlabrendorff, *Offiziere*, 26.

39. Ibid., 24.

40. Edmund Forschbach, *Edgar J. Jung* (Tübingen: Neske, 1984), 37.

41. Cartarius, *Widerstand*, 76.

42. Zeller, *Flame*, 216, from a letter dated 23 August 1941.

43. Schlabrendorff, *Offiziere*, 72.

44. Müller, *Oberst*, 170.

45. Reynolds, *Treason*, 208. The conversation was with Pastor Helmut Gollwitzer in the summer of 1940.

46. Müller, *Oberst*, 400.

47. The comments were made in the summer of 1942. See Kramarz, *Stauffenberg*, 116; Zeller, *Flame*, 424.

48. Schlabrendorff, *Offiziere*, 35.

49. Bethge, *Bonhoeffer*, 325.

50. Roon, *Ordnung*, 177. Delp was speaking at a 1943 conference on care for wounded soldiers; his comments suggest, however, a wider interpretation.

51. Lill, *20. Juli*, 233.

52. Thun-Hohenstein, *Der Verschwörer*, 92.

53. Hassell, *Tagebücher*, 71, entry for 12 December 1938; 85, entry for 22 March 1939; 152, entry for 25 December 1939; 164, entry for 14–17 February 1940; 210, entry for 8 October 1940; 240, entry for 29 March 1940. "Nostitz," mentioned in the Christmas, 1939 entry, was "Gogo" Mostitz, one of Hassell's many contacts in the Foreign Office.

54. Balfour, *Moltke*, 80.

55. Balfour, *Moltke*, 172. Also Zeller, *Flame*, 412. The previous spring, in May 1940, Moltke went through a period of profound depression, a depression from which he never fully recovered. See Balfour's comments in *Moltke*, 122.

56. Scheurig, *Tresckow*, 124.

57. Bethge, *Bonhoeffer*, 379.

58. Bonhoeffer, *Prayers*, 44. The poems mentioned can be found in *Prayers*, 27–28 and 33–35.

59. Müller, *Oberst*, 283.

60. Zeller, *Flame*, 77.

61. Cited in *Bekenntnis*, 90.

62. Zeller, *Flame*, 413.

63. Bethge, *Bonhoeffer*, 736.

64. Yorck, *Stärke*, 70.

65. Scheurig, *Tresckow*, 192.

66. Ibid., 195.

67. Hoffmann, *Widerstand gegen Hitler*, 67.

68. Kramarz, *Stauffenberg*, 128.

69. Finker, *Stauffenberg*, 356.

70. Reynolds, *Treason*, 245.

71. Müller, *Oberst*, 429.

72. Zimmermann, *I Knew*, 194, 203. Bonhoeffer made these remarks while visiting Stockholm, on a mission from the Abwehr.

73. Lill, *20. Juli*, 132.

74. Foerster, *Beck*, 164.

75. Reynolds, *Treason*, 241.

76. Ibid., 239.

77. Ibid., 255.

78. Bonhoeffer, *Ethics*, 75.

79. Vassiltchikov, *Diaries*, 204.

Chapter 7. Gewissen

1. Helmuth James von Moltke, *Briefe an Freya* (Munich: Beck, 1988), 39.

2. Raul Hilberg, *The Destruction of the European Jews* (New York: Watts, 1973), 719.

3. Vassiltchikov, *Diaries*, 67.

4. Reck-Malleczewen, *Diary*, 166.

5. Hassell, *Tagebücher*, 337, entry for 13 November 1942.

6. Bethge, *Bonhoeffer*, 659.

7. Bonhoeffer, *Letters*, 3. Citations follow, in general, this translation; occasional modifications are bawed on the German original, which may be found in Dietrich Bonhoeffer, *Widerstand und Ergebung* (Munich: Kaiser, 1951), 9–25.

8. Bonhoeffer, *Letters*, 3.

9. Ibid., 5–6.

10. Ibid., 11.

11. Ibid., 16.

12. Ibid., 5.

13. Moltke, *Briefe*, 610.

14. This distinction between ideas and interests, and between action and behavior, is discussed in a wide range of literature. Hannah Arendt identifies "acting" as a distinctive human characteristic in her study, *The Human Condition* (Chicago: University of Chicago Press, 1958), 7ff. For commentary on Arendt, see Lean Bradshaw, *Acting and Thinking* (Toronto: University of Toronto, 1989), 10ff; George Kateb, *Hannah Arendt* (New York: Rowman and Allanheld, 1984), 22 ff. Christopher Lasch develops the distinction between ideas and interests and action and behavior in his *The True and Only Heaven* (New York: Norton, 1991), 133ff. Clifford Geertz clearly and effectively defends the notion of the relative autonomy of "mind" in his essay, "The Growth and Culture and the Evolution of Mind," in Clifford Geertz, *The Interpretation of Cultures* (New York: Basic Books, 1973), 55–83. For an introduction to the relationship between ideas and values and politics, see Robert Nisbet, *Twilight of Authority* (New York: Oxford, 1975), 9ff.

15. John Maynard Keynes, *The General Theory of Employment, Interest, and Money* (New York: Harcourt, Brace, and World, 1964), 383.

16. Ernst Bloch, *A Philosophy of the Future*, trans. John Cumming (New York: Herder and Herder, 1970), 19.

17. Bonhoeffer, *Letters*, 8–9.

18. Fest, *Hitler*, 376–77.

19. Peter Haas, *Morality after Auschwitz* (Philadelphia: Fortress, 1988), 2.

20. Joseph H. Berke, *The Tyranny of Malice* (New York: Summit, 1988). See also Ricoeur, *Symbolism of Evil*; Ernest Becker, *The Structure of Evil* (New York: Braziller, 1968); Erich Fromm, *The Anatomy of Human Destructiveness* (New York: Fawcett, 1973).

21. Bonhoeffer, *Letters*, 4.

22. Moltke, *Briefe*, 33.

23. See discussion in chapter 6, Anti-Christ.

24. Bonhoeffer discusses the "orders of preservation," or the "namdates," in, for example, his *Ethics*, 207ff. For a detailed commentary on Bonhoeffer's notion of the "orders of preservation," see James Burtness, *Shaping the Future. The Ethics of Dietrich Bonhoeffer* (Philadelphia: Fortress, 1985), 85ff.

25. Bonhoeffer, *Letters*, 12–13.

26. Moltke, *Briefe*, 35.

27. Bonhoeffer, *Letters*, 11. Bonhoeffer repeatedly questions the notion that God is "up there" or "out there" in his prison letters. See, for example, his famous letter of 30 April 1944, in *Letters*, 278. See also Burtness's discussion in *Shaping*, 54 ff.

28. Bonhoeffer, *Letters*, 7.

29. Ibid., 15.

30. Kurt Meier, *Der Evangelische Kirchenkampf* (Göttingen: Vanderhoeck and Ruprecht, 1984), 190–91.

31. Yorck, *Stärke*, 154.

32. Paul Tillich, *Morality and Beyond* (New York: Harper and Row, 1963), 19.

33. Ibid., 20–21.

34. Ibid., 67.
35. Ibid., 77.
36. Ibid., 78.
37. Bonhoeffer, *Letters*, 4.
38. Tillich, *Morality*, 59.
39. Ibid., 77.
40. Ibid., 77.
41. Ibid., 79.
42. This is a recurring theme in Bonhoeffer's work. See, for example, Dietrich Bonhoeffer, *Nachfolge* (Munich: Kaiser, 1937), 65, translated by R. H. Fuller as *The Cost of Discipleship*; also Bonhoeffer, *Ethics*, 75–79; 218ff.
43. Bonhoeffer, *Letters*, 16.
44. Alasdair MacIntyre, *After Virtue: An Essay in Moral Theory* (South Bend, Ind.: Notre Dame, 1981), 30ff.
45. Bethge, *Bonhoeffer*, 1037. Bonhoeffer made the remark, in English, to an English fellow-prisoner, Payne Best. Bonhoeffer asked Best to remember him to Anglican Bishop George Bell, Bonhoeffer's old friend. Payne remembered that Bonhoeffer said: "Tell him that for me this is the end, but also the beginning."
46. Reinhold Niebuhr, *Beyond Tragedy* (New York: Scribners, 1965), 115.
47. Ibid., 279,
48. Ibid., 283.
49. Ibid., 277.
50. Bonhoeffer, *Letters*, 17.
51. Ibid., 369–70.

Epitaph: Gewitteraktion

1. All of the standard biographies of Hitler include information concerning his injuries. See, for example, John Toland, *Adolf Hitler* (New York: Doubleday, 1976), 815–18; Alan Bullock, *Hitler: A Study in Tyranny* (New York: Harper and Row, 1964), 744; Fest, *Hitler*, 708.
2. Albert Speer, *Inside the Third Reich* (New York: Macmillan, 1970), 389–90. The "Sonderkommission 20. Juli," the "July 20th Special Commission," included some four hundred officials, sorted into eleven different groups. By the end of the war, they had ordered around seven thousand arrests—see Finker, *Stauffenberg*, 344. The official Gestapo report on 20 July was published some two decades after the war, amid great controversy, entitled *Spiegelbild einer Verschwörung*, ed. Hans-Adolf Jacobson (Stuttgart: Seewald, 1984). *Spiegelbild* provides important primary evidence, but, given its Gestapo authors, it must be used cautiously.
3. See Georg Holmsten, *Deutschland, July 1944* (Dusseldorf: Droste, 1982), 127 ff.
4. Fest, *Hitler*, 712.
5. Speer, *Inside*, 390.
6. Heinz Boberach, ed., *Meldungen aus dem Reich* (Berlin: Pawlik, 1984), 6684.
7. Hastings, *Overlord*, 279.
8. Finker, *Stauffenberg*, 361.
9. Hoffmann, *Opposition*, 526.

10. Cartarius, *Widerstand,* 265.

11. Balfour, *Moltke,* 320ff.

12. The farewell letters of German resisters were published as Helmut Goll-witzer, ed., *Du hast mich heimgesucht bei Nacht* (Muncih: Kaiser, 1980). Citations are from Hassell, 57; Haeften, 107; and Yorck, 90.

13. Fest, *Hitler,* 712.

14. These ghastly films were destroyed by the end of the war, though rumors persist that copies may have survived. Albert Speer recalls seeing photographs of the hanged men that summer of 1944. Speer writes: "During these days a heap of photographs also lay on [Hitler's] table. Lost in thought, I picked one up, but quickly put it down. It was a picture of a hanged man, in convict dress, a broad, colored stripe on his trousers. One of the SS leaders standing near me remarked in explanation, 'that's Witzleben. Don't you want to see the others too? These are all photos of the executions.' That evening the film of the execution of the conspirators was shown in the movie room. I could not and would not see it. But in order not to attract attention, I gave the excuse that I was far behind in my work. I saw many others going to this showing, mostly lower-ranking SS men and civilians. Not a single officer of the Wehrmacht attended." Speer, *Inside,* 395. At Plötzensee Prison in Berlin, where many of the July 20 Conspirators were executed, thin rope or wire was attached to hooks in an overhead beam; the condemned man, usually naked, was lifted so that his head entered the rope or wire, and then released. The condemned man would die of slow strangulation, and some took many minutes to die. Plötzensee also had a guillotine, and some of the condemned men were beheaded. Plötzensee is now a memorial. See Hoffman, *History,* 528.

15. Fest, *Hitler,* 716.

16. Bethge, *Bonhoeffer,* 1037.

17. Schlabrendorff, *Offiziere,* 153.

18. There are several accounts of this strange little convoy. See, for instance, Schlabrendorff, *Offiziere,* 157; Leon Blum, *L'oeuvre* (Paris: Edition Albin Michel, 1955), vol. 5, 540–42; Hjalmar Schacht, *76 Jahre Meines Lebens* (Bad Wornishofen: Kindler and Schiermeyer, 1953), 553–55; also Joel Colton, *Leon Blum* (New York: Knopf, 1966), 443–44; James Bentley, *Martin Niemoeller* (New York: Free Press, 1984), 155.

19. The Americans were not too pleased with Schlabrendorff's account; it certainly seemed to blur the easy judgment that all Germans were somehow Nazis. In the immediate postwar years, the American authorities were more interested in "de-Nazification" than in understanding German anti-Nazis. The Americans prohibited the publication of Schlabrendorff's book in their sector of Germany, and Schlabrendorff had to bring the first edition of the book out in Switzerland.

20. Fest, *Hitler,* 669, 716.

21. William Faulkner, "The Bear," in *The Portable Faulkner* (New York: Viking, 1946), 204.

22. Dietrich Bonhoeffer, *Prayers from Prison* (Philadelphia: Fortress, 1983), 25.

23. C. S. Lewis, *The World's Last Night* (New York: Harcourt Brace Jovanovich, 1959), 10–11.

Bibliography

The essential bibliographic guide to the German resistance and the 20 July plot is Ulrich Cartarius, and the Forschungsgemeinschaft 20. Juli, ed., *Bibliographie 'Widerstand'* (Munich: Saur, 1984), which lists some 6,231 publications. The most complete list of available primary sources can be found in Peter Hoffman, *Widerstand—Staatsstreich—Attentat* (Munich: Piper, 1970), published in English as Peter Hoffmann, *The German Resistance to Hitler* (New York: MacMillan, 1979).

Primary Sources

Barth, Karl. *Ethics*. Translated by Geoffrey W. Bromiley. New York: Seabury, 1981.

Bethge, Eberhard, ed. *Last Letters of Resistance: Farewells from the Bonhoeffer Family*. Translated by Dennis Slabaugh. Philadelphia: Fortress, 1984.

Boberach, Heinz, ed. *Meldungungen aus dem Reich: Die geheimen Lageberichte des Sicherheitsdienstes der SS, 1938–1945*. 17 volumes. Berlin: Pawlak, 1984.

Bonhoeffer, Dietrich. *Christ the Center*. Translated by Edwin Robertson. New York: Harper and Row, 1978.

———. *The Cost of Discipleship*. Translated by R. H. Fuller. New York: Macmillan, 1972. Originally published as *Nachfolge*. Munich: Kaiser, 1937.

———. *Creation and Fall*. Translated by John Fletcher. New York: Macmillan, 1959.

———. *Ethics*. Translated by N. H. Smith. New York: Macmillan, 1955. Originally published as *Ethik*, edited by Eberhard Bethge. Munich: Kaiser, 1949.

———. *Fiction from Prison*. Translated by Ursula Hoffmann. Philadelphia: Fortress, 1981.

———. *Letters and Papers from Prison*. Translated by Reginald Fuller, et al. New York: Macmillan, 1972. Originally published as *Widerstand und Ergebung*, edited by Eberhard Bethge. Munich: Kaiser, 1970.

———. *Life Together*. Translated by John Doberstein. New York: Harper and Row, 1954.

———. *Prayers from Prison*. Translated by Johann Hampe. Philadelphia: Fortress, 1983.

———. *Spiritual Care*. Translated by Jay Rochelle. Philadelphia: Fortress, 1985.

Casey, William. *The Secret War Against Hitler*. New York: Berkley, 1989.

Dulles, Allen. *Germany's Underground*. New York: Macmillan, 1947.

Europäische Publikationen. *Die Vollmacht des Gewissens*. Munich: Rinn, 1957.

Fritzsche, Hans Karl. *Ein Leben im Schatten des Verrates*. Freiburg: Herder, 1984.

Fromm, Bella. *Blood and Banquets: A Berlin Social Diary*. New York: Harpers, 1942.

Gisevius, Hans Bernd. *Bis zum bitteren Ende*. Frankfurt: Knaur, 1982.

Gollwitzer, Helmut, ed. *Du hast mich heimgesucht bei Nacht*. Munich: Kaiser, 1980.

Hagen, Hans. *Zwischen Eid und Befehl*. Munich: Turmer, 1964.

von Hammerstein, Kunrat. *Flucht: Aufzeichnungen nach dem 20. Juli*. Freiburg: Walter, 1966.

von Hassell, Ulrich. *Die Hassell-Tagebücher, 1938–1944*. Berlin: Siedler, 1988.

Haushofer, Albrecht. *Moabit Sonnets*. Translated by M. D. Herter Norton. New York: Norton, 1978.

von Horvath, Odon. *Sladek oder die Schwarze Armee*. Frankfurt: Suhrkamp, 1978.

John, Otto. *"Falsch und zu Spät."* Berlin: Ullstein, 1989.

von Moltke, Helmuth James. *Briefe an Freya*. Munich: Beck, 1988.

Niemoeller, Martin. *Exile in the Fatherland*. Edited by Hubert Locke. Grand Rapids, Mich.: Eerdmanns, 1986.

Peter, Kral-Heinrich, ed. *Spiegelbild einer Verschwörung: Die Kaltenbrunner-Berichte an Bormann und Hitler über das Attentat von 20. Juli 1944*. Stuttgart: Seewald, 1961.

Reck-Malleczewen, Friedrich. *Diary of a Man in Despair*. Translated by Paul Rubens. New York: Macmillan, 1970.

Remer, Otto Ernst. *Verschwörung und Verrat um Hitler*. Preussisch Oldendorf: Schutz, 1984.

Scheurig, Bobo, ed. *Deutscher Widerstand 1938–1944. Dokumente*. Munich: Deutscher Taschenbuch, 1984.

von Schlabrendorff, Fabian. *Offiziere gegen Hitler*. Berlin: Siedler, 1984.

Scholder, Klaus, ed. *Die Mittwochgesellschaft: Protokolle aus dem geistigen Deutschland, 1932 bis 1944*. Berlin: Severin and Siedler, 1982.

von Seekt, Hans. *Antikes Feldherrntum*. Berlin: 1929.

Speer, Albert. *Inside the Third Reich*. Translated by Richard and Clara Winston. New York: Macmillan, 1970.

Stahlberg, Alexander. *Die verdamnmte Pflicht*. Berlin: Ullstein, 1990.

Stieff, Helmuth. *Briefe*. Berlin: Siedler, 1991.

Vassiltchikov, Marie. *Berlin Diaries, 1940–1945*. New York: Knopf, 1987.

Warlimont, Walter. *Inside Hitler's Headquarters*. Translated by R. H. Barry. New York: Praeger, 1964.

Yorck von Wartenburg, Marion. *Die Stärke der Stille*. Cologne: Eugen Diederich, 1984.

Zuckmayer, Carl. *Des Teufels General*, in *Gesammelte werke*, vol. 3. Frankfurt: Fischer, 1960.

Zuckmayer, Carl. *A Part of Myself.* Translated by Richard and Clara Winston. New York: Harcourt Brace Jovanovich, 1966.

Secondary Sources

Arendt, Hannah. *Eichmann in Jerusalem.* New York: Viking, 1964.

Balfour, Michael. *Helmuth James von Moltke.* London: Macmillan, 1972.

Barker, Ernest. *Traditions of Civility.* New York: Archon, 1967.

Beck, Dorothea. *Julius Leber: Sozialdemokrat zwischen Reform und Widerstand.* Berlin: Siedler, 1983.

Bekenntnis und Verpflichtung: Reden und Aufsätze zur zehnjährigen Wiederkehr des 20. Juli 1944. Stuttgart: Friedrich Vorwerk, 1955.

Bentley, James. *Martin Niemoeller.* New York: Free Press, 1984.

Bergsdorf, Wolfgang. "Der ermordete Ghostwriter." *Die Zeit,* 6 July 1984, p. 9.

Besier, Gerhard, and Gerhard Ringshausen, eds. *Bekenntnis, Widerstand, Martyrium.* Göttingen: Vanderhoeck and Ruprecht, 1986.

Bessell, Richard. *Political Violence and the Rise of Nazism.* New Haven: Yale University Press, 1984.

Bethge, Eberhard. *Costly Grace.* New York: Harper and Row, 1979.

———. *Dietrich Bonhoeffer.* Munich: Kaiser, 1983.

Bielenberg, Christabel. *Christabel.* New York: Penguin, 1989.

Bloch, Ernst. *A Philosophy of the Future.* Translated by John Cumming, New York; Herder and Herder, 1970.

Bucheler, Heinrich. *Carl-Heinrich von Stülpnagel.* Berlin: Ullstein, 1989.

Breit, Gotthard. *Das Staats- und Gesellschaftsbild deutscher Generäle beider Weltkriege im Spiegel ihrer Memoiren.* Boppard: Boldt, 1973.

Buchheit, Gert. *Richter in roter Robe: Freisler, Präsident des Volksgerichtshofes.* Munich: List, 1968.

Burtness, James. *Shaping the Future: The Ethics of Dietrich Bonhoeffer.* Philadelphia: Fortress, 1985.

Cartarius, Ulrich. *Deutscher Widerstand.* Berlin: Siedler, 1984.

Coleman, John. "The Christian as Citizen." *Commonweal,* 9 September 1983, pp. 457–62.

Colton, Joel. *Leon Blum: Humanist in Politics.* New York: Knopf, 1966.

Cooper, Matthew. *The German Army, 1933–1945.* New York: Bonanza, 1984.

Dahrendorff, Ralf. *Society and Democracy in Germany.* New York: Doubleday, 1969.

Demeter, Karl. *Das Deutsche Offizierkorps in Gesellschaft und Staat.* Frankfurt: Graefe, 1962.

Deutsch, Harold. *The Conspiracy against Hitler in the Twilight War.* Minneapolis: University of Minnesota Press, 1968.

———. *Hitler and his Generals. The Hidden Crisis, January–June, 1938.* Minneapolis: University of Minnesota Press, 1974.

Ehlers, Dieter. *Technik und Moral einer Verschwörung.* Frankfurt: Atheneum, 1964.

Eschenburg, Theodor. "Das obsolete Ehrenwort." *Die Zeit*, 10 February 1984, p. 4.

Feil, Ernst. *The Theology of Dietrich Bonhoeffer*. Philadelphia: Fortress, 1985.

Fest, Joachim. *Hitler*. Translated by Richard and Clara Winston. New York: Vintage, 1975.

Finker, Klaus. *Stauffenberg und der 20. Juli 1944*. Cologne: Pahl-Rugenstein, 1977.

Foerster, Wolfgang. *Generaloberst Ludwig Beck*. Munich: Isar, 1953.

Forschbach, Edmund. *Edgar J. Jung: ein konservativer Revolutionär*. Tübingen: Neske, 1984.

Fox, Richard. *Reinhold Niebuhr*. New York: Pantheon, 1985.

Frevert. Ute. *Ehrenmänner: Das Duell in der bürgerlichen Gesellschaft*. Munich: Beck, 1991.

Galante, Pierre. *Operation Valkyrie*. New York: Dell, 1981.

Gallin, Mother Mary Alice. *Ethical and Religious Factors in the German Resistance to Hitler*. Washington, D.C.: Catholic University Press, 1955.

Giordano, Ralph. *Die zweite Schuld*. Munich: Knaur, 1990.

Girard, Rene. *Violence and the Sacred*. Baltimore, Md.: Johns Hopkins University Press, 1979.

Gleichen-Russwurm, Alexander. *Schiller*. Stuttgart: Julius Hoffmann, 1913.

Godsey, John. *The Theology of Dietrich Bonhoeffer*. Philadelphia: Westminster, 1959.

Graml, Hermann, ed. *Widerstand im Dritten Reich*. Frankfurt: Fischer, 1984.

Greene, James, and John Donlon, eds. *The Essential Thomas More*. New York: Mentor, 1967.

Gross, Miriam. "Why the 'Good' Germans Failed." *London Sunday Times*, 22 July 1984, p. 33.

Hartman, Geoffrey. *Bitburg in Moral and Political Perspective*. Bloomington: Indiana University Press, 1986.

von Hassell, Fey. *Hostage of the Third Reich*. New York: Scribner's, 1989.

Hastings, Max. *Overlord*. New York: Simon and Schuster, 1984.

Hohne, Heinz. *Canaris*. Munich: Bertelsmann, 1984.

Hoffman, Peter. *Hitler's Personal Security*. Cambridge: MIT Press, 1979.

——. *Widerstand gegen Hitler*. Munich: Piper, 1979.

——. *Widerstand—Staatsstreich—Attentat*. Munich: Piper, 1970.

Holmsten, Georg. *Deutschland Juli 1944*. Düsseldorf: Droste, 1982.

Hubertus zu Lowenstein, Prince. *What Was the German Resistance Movement?* Bad Godesberg: Grafes, 1965.

Irving, David. *The Trail of the Fox*. New York: Avon, 1977.

Kateb, George. *Hannah Arendt. Politics, Conscience, Evil*. Totowa, N.J.: Rowman and Allanheld, 1984.

Kramarz, Joachim. *Stauffenberg*. New York: Macmillan, 1967.

Lasch, Christopher. *The Culture of Narcissism*. New York: Norton, 1978.

——. *The Minimal Self*. New York: Norton, 1984.

——. *The True and Only Heaven*. New York: Norton, 1991.

Lewis, C. S. *The World's Last Night.* New York: Harcourt Brace Jovanovich, 1959.

Liddell Hart, B. H. *The German Generals Talk.* New York: Quill, 1979.

Lill, Rudolf, and Heinrich Oberreuter, eds. *20. Juli.* Düsseldorf: Econ, 1984.

Löwenthal, Richard, and Patrik von zur Muhlen, eds. *Widerstand und Verweigerung in Deutschland, 1933 bis 1945.* Bonn: Dietz, 1982.

Malone, Harry. *Adam von Trott zu Solz.* Berlin: Siedler, 1986.

Manvell, Roger, and Heinrich Fraenkel. *The Men Who Tried to Kill Hitler.* New York: Pocket Books, 1966.

Markmann, Hans-Jochen. *Der deutsche Widerstand gegen den Nationalsozialismus 1933–1945: Modelle für den Unterricht.* Mainz: Hase and Koehler, 1984.

Meier, Kurt. *Der evangelische Kirchenkampf.* Göttingen: Vandenhoeck and Ruprecht, 1976.

Meyer-Krahmer, Marianne. *Carl Goerderler.* Freiburg: Herder, 1989.

Militärgeschichtliches Forschungsamt. *Das Deutsche Reich und der Zweite Weltkrieg.* Stuttgart: Deutsche Verlags-Anstalt, 1979.

———. *Aufstand des Gewissens.* Bonn: Mittler and Sohn, 1985.

"Misplaced Gratitude." *The New Republic,* 13 and 20 August 1984, p. 8.

Müller, Christian. *Oberst i.G. Stauffenberg.* Düsseldorf: Droste, 1971.

Müller, Klaus-Jürgen. *Armee, Politik, und Gesellschaft in Deutschland, 1933–1945.* Paderborn: Schöningh, 1979.

"New Perspectives on the German Resistance against National Socialism." Articles by Harold Deutsch, Peter Hoffmann, Klemens von Klemperer, Robert Paxton, and Leonidas Hill. *Central European History* 14, no. 4 (December 1981).

Niebuhr, Reinhold. *Beyond Tragedy.* New York: Scribner's, 1965.

O'Neill, Robert. *The German Army and the Nazi Party.* London: Corgi, 1966.

Paine, Lauran. *German Military Intelligence in World War II.* New York: Stein and Day, 1984.

Pentzlin, Heinz. *Hjalmar Schacht.* Frankfurt: Ullstein, 1980.

Reed, T. J. *The Classical Center.* London: Croom Helm, 1980.

Reynolds, Nicholas. *Treason Was No Crime.* London: William Kimber, 1979.

Ricoeur, Paul. *The Symbolism of Evil.* Translated by Emerson Buchanan. Boston: Beacon, 1967.

Rings, Werner. *Life with the Enemy.* New York: Doubleday, 1982.

Ritter, Gerhard. *Carl Goerdeler und die deutsche Widerstandsbewegung.* Stuttgart: Deutsche Verlags-Anstalt, 1984.

———. *Frederick the Great.* Berkeley: University of California Press, 1968.

———. *The German Resistance.* New York: Praeger, 1958.

Romoser, George. "The Politics of Uncertainty: The German Resistance Movement." *Social Research* 31 (1964): p. 73.

Rothfels, Hans. *Deutsche Opposition gegen Hitler.* Frankfurt: Fischer, 1986.

van Roon, Ger. *Neuordnung im Widerstand.* Munich: Oldenbourg, 1967.

———. *Widerstand im Dritten Reich.* Munich: Beck, 1979.

Rouette, Hans-Peter. *Die Widerstandslegende*. Berlin: Inaugural Dissertation, Free University of Berlin, 1983.

Scheurig, Bodo. *Henning von Tresckow*. Frankfurt: Ullstein, 1980.

———. *Freies Deutschland. Das Nationalkomitee und der Bund Deutscher Offiziere in der Sowjetunion, 1943–1945*. Cologne: Kiepenheuer and Witsch, 1984.

Schmädecke, Jürgen and Peter Steinbach, eds. *Der Widerstand gegen den Nationalsozialismus*. Munich: Piper, 1985.

Schmitthenner, Walter, and Hans Buchheim, eds. *Der deutsche Widerstand gegen Hitler*. Cologne: Kiepenheuer and Witsch, 1966.

Schultz, Gerhard, ed. *Geheimdienste und Widerstandsbewegungen im Zweiten Weltkrieg*. Göttingen: Vandenhoeck and Ruprecht, 1982.

von Schwerin, Detlef. *"Dann sind's die besten Köpfe, die Man Henkt."* Munich: Piper, 1991.

Sennett, Richard. *The Fall of Public Man*. New York: Vintage, 1976.

Severin, Pitt, and Hartmut Jetter. *25 Jahre Bundesrepublik Deutschland*. Munich: Fritz Molden, 1974.

Spires, David. *Image and Reality: The Making of the German Officer, 1921–1933*. Westport, Conn.: Greenwood, 1984.

Stern, J. P. *Hitler: The Führer and the People*. Berkeley: University of California Press, 1975.

Stumpf, Reinhard. *Die Wehrmacht-Elite*. Boppard: Boldt, 1982.

Sykes, Christopher. *Tormented Loyalty*. New York: Harper and Row, 1969.

Tauber, Kurt. *Beyond Eagle and Swastika: German nationalism since 1945*. Middletown, Conn.: Wesleyan University Press, 1967.

Taylor, Telford. *Sword and Swastika*. Chicago: Quadrangle, 1952.

von Thun-Hohenstein, Romedio Galeazzo. *Der Verschwörer*. Berlin: Severin and Siedler, 1982.

Tillich, Paul. *Morality and Beyond*. New York: Harper and Row, 1963.

Venohr, Wolfgang. *Stauffenberg*. Frankfurt: Ullstein, 1986.

von Voss, Rüdiger, and Günter Neske, eds. *Der 20. Juli 1944*. Augsburg: Neske, 1984.

Wheeler-Bennett, John. *The Nemesis of Power*. New York: St. Martin's, 1954.

Wilkinson, James. *The Intellectual Resistance in Europe*. Cambridge: Harvard University Press, 1981.

Wright, Derek. *The Psychology of Moral Behavior*. New York: Penguin, 1971.

Zeller, Eberhard. *The Flame of Freedom*. London: Wolff, 1967.

Zentner, Kurt. *Illustrierte Geschichte des Widerstands in Deutschland und Europa, 1933–1945*. Munich: Südwest, 1966.

Zimmermann, Wolf-Dieter, and Ronald Smith, eds. *I Knew Dietrich Bonhoeffer*. New York: Harper and Row, 1966.

Index